Better Homes and Gardens®

gifts
from the
heart™

A year-round
collection of gifts
for handcrafters of
all ages to make
with pride and give
with love!

Stencils and paint, scissors and fabric, paper and pen,
rubber stamps and ink, needle and thread—
all these materials and more—combine to make wonderful
handmade gifts for every occasion from a first home to
a new baby, from Valentine's Day to Christmas.

Better Homes and Gardens®

gifts
from the
heart™

Better Homes and Gardens® Creative Collection
Des Moines, Iowa

VOLUME 1

handmade gifts

Opportunities to give handcrafted presents—

Gifts from the Heart™*—happen every day of the year.*

Handmade gifts are natural for Valentine's Day,

Mother's Day, Father's Day, and all the occasions

that show up on the calendar. Sometimes a dinner invitation,

special help from a teacher, the appearance of a new

neighbor, or a random kindness suggests an impromptu

gift in return. A once-in-a-lifetime wedding, graduation,

or christening demands a gift to match the

uniqueness of the celebration.

This collection was created to commemorate all of life's

sharing times—from spur-of-the-moment to planned-for-

months events. Turn the pages of this book to find

handcrafted heirlooms for life's big dates, simple projects to

celebrate the seasons, little gifts for no reason, and

handmade items to give every day of the year.

When you craft these projects with pride and give them

with love, they are truly Gifts from the Heart.

A gift of memories, whether it's a scrapbook or a pretty collection of family treasures, will be cherished for a lifetime.

TABLE OF CONTENTS

Silk Hydrangea Wreath starts on *page 14*.

Punched Paper Lace starts on *page 14*.

Occasions for giving *tokens of love* and friendship arise every day of the year. *Why wait for February?*

In this *romantic* collection, a virtual bouquet of hearts-and-flowers mementos abounds. *Handcraft* them from paper, dried flowers, and paint. Or, *stitch* them up in appliqué and embroidery.

TOKENS OF
love,
AND
friend

ship

**Old Friend Pillow
starts on *page 16.***

"Heart" pressed for a friendship gift? It's at your fingertips.
Just dig through your *fabrics,* untangle those flosses,
and dust off the button jar. In a matter of stitches, you'll have
a present as *unique* as the special friend in mind.

**Glittering Valentines
start on *page 17.***

Handmade valentines *share* love and friendship
anytime of year! Reach for some rubber-stamping supplies
to create a *heartfelt* message. Enclose sparkly glitter,
charms, and buttons in a see-through shaker
made from a *rubber-stamp* template.

Felt Heart Mat
starts on *page 18.*

Stitch your *kindest* regards into this warm and woolly heart-trimmed table mat. Perfect for a housewarming or host's gift, the *Amish-style* design is done in *felt* and appliqued all over with blanket stitches.

Blue Roses Trinket
starts on *page 19.*

With a few freehand strokes, *blue roses* come to full *bloom* on this painted wood trinket. About 8 inches tall, it's certain to set someone's heart *glowing.*

punched paper lace

Shown *opposite* and on *page 9*.

MATERIALS

For the doily

- 1 sheet of typing paper
- 14" square of thin rice paper
- Decorative paper punches:
  Jumbo Craft Punch 1"-wide daisy,
  All Night Media ⅝"-wide flower, and
  1"-wide four-hearts
- Small circle hole punch
- 8 Beadery elongated 13×6mm bicone,
  small hole crystal beads
- 32 Beadery 4mm round, small hole
  crystal beads
- 1 package Mill Hill Ice glass seed
  beads #02010
- White sewing thread
- Beading needle

For the fan

- 1 sheet of typing paper
- 4½×14" strip of thin rice paper
- Ruler
- Jumbo Craft Punch 1"-wide daisy
  paper punch
- Small circle paper punch
- Mill Hill Tea Rose glass seed beads
  #02004
- Mill Hill Sea Breeze small bugle
  beads #72008
- White sewing thread
- Beading needle
- 2 yards of ¹³/₁₆"-wide white silk ribbon

For the candy papers

- Cupcake and candy papers
- Small star and small circle paper
  punches

INSTRUCTIONS

Trace the desired pattern on *page 15*
onto a piece of typing paper. Cut
out the pattern, including the shaded
portions, using the decorative and
hole punches. Set the patterns aside.

silk hydrangea wreath

Wreath measures 10" in diameter. Shown *above* and on *page 8*.

MATERIALS

- 10"-diameter heart-shaped
  grapevine wreath
- 1 stem of silk cream hydrangea with
  large and small petals
- 1 dried bunch *each* of Knud Nielsen
  green hops, pink gomphrena, and
  dark red cockscomb
- 1 bunch of artificial light green grapes
- Glue gun and hotmelt adhesive

INSTRUCTIONS

Cut individual large and small flower
heads from the cream hydrangea
stem. Randomly glue the flower
heads onto the front and sides of the
grapevine wreath to cover.

Cut small pieces of dark red
cockscomb and individual flower
heads of green hops and pink
gomphrena. Cut groups of two or
three grapes. Glue these around the
wreath at random intervals in a
pleasing arrangement. ❤

Designer: Lorna Call
Photographer: Perry Struse

necessary to complete the design. Punch out the shaded portions first, then cut along the outlines.

Following the pattern, sew the seed and bugle beads to the fan using a single strand of white thread. Thread silk ribbon through the punched holes along the bottom edge of the fan; tie a bow.

candy papers

Randomly punch small stars and circles into the sides of the papers. ❤

Designer: Laura Collins
Photographer: Scott Little

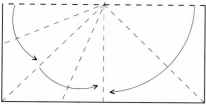

Folding diagram

Trace the pattern onto one side of the folded paper shape. For best results, punch through only two or three folds/layers of the paper at a time, retracing the pattern as

doily

Fold the rice paper in quarters; open up the last fold (the square will be folded in half). Referring to the diagram, *above*, fold the half-square into eighths. Trace the pattern onto one side of the folded paper shape.

Align and punch with the shaded areas first. Then trim the outer edge For best results, punch through two or three folds/layers of paper at a time, retracing the pattern as necessary to complete the designs.

Following the pattern, sew the round crystal beads and the seed beads to the doily using a single strand of white thread. Sew a round crystal bead and an elongated bicone crystal bead to each point of the octagon-shaped doily.

fan

Carefully mark dots at 1⅝" intervals along the long edges of the 4½×14" rice paper strip. Fold the strip in accordion pleats, matching the dots.

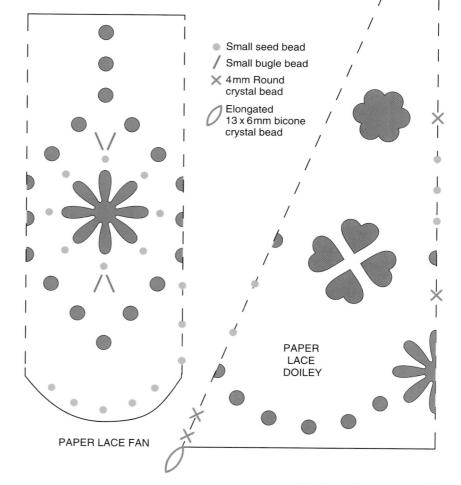

● Small seed bead
╱ Small bugle bead
✕ 4mm Round crystal bead
⬭ Elongated 13 x 6mm bicone crystal bead

PAPER LACE DOILEY

PAPER LACE FAN

old friend pillow

Finished pillow measures 14"-square. Shown on *page 10*.

MATERIALS

- ⅜ yard of 45"-wide cotton duck or unbleached muslin
- 4—⅛ yard pieces of 45"-wide homespun plaid
- Tracing paper
- Black iron-on transfer pen
- Brown, green, blue, red, burgundy, peach, and black cotton embroidery floss
- Size 26 chenille needle
- 14"-square pillow form
- Approximately 6 dozen vintage-looking buttons

BACKSTITCH
- Brown
- Green
- Blue
- Red
- Burgundy
- Peach
- Black

CROSS-STITCH
- ✕ Burgundy

FRENCH KNOT
- • Red
- • Black

STRAIGHT STITCH
- ╱ Red

INSTRUCTIONS

All measurements include a ¼" seam allowance. Seams are sewn with right sides together unless otherwise specified.

From the cotton duck, cut a square approximately 13½×13½" for the pillow face. (Set the remaining duck fabric aside.) Place the tracing paper over the pattern, *opposite,* and trace it using the iron-on transfer pen. Center the traced pattern, ink side down, on the duck square and transfer according to manufacturer's instructions.

Using the photograph on *page 10* as a guide, complete the embroidery using three plies of floss and a chenille needle. To give the design a primitive look, don't follow the lines exactly and use irregular backstitches. Use three plies of floss wrapped twice around the needle to complete the French knots.

When all the stitching is complete, press the stitched piece face down on a soft towel. Centering the stitching, trim the piece to 9" square.

From the remaining cotton duck, cut two 14½×10" rectangles for the pillow back. From two of the homespun plaids, cut a 3¼×9" border strip. From each of the remaining homespun plaids, cut a 3¼×14½" border strip. Sew one 3¼×9" border strip to the top edge of the stitched piece and one to the bottom. Press the seams toward the homespun strips. Sew a 3¼×14½" border strip to each side of the stitched piece. Press the seams toward the homespun strips. Press the completed pillow top carefully. It should measure 14½" square.

Hem one long edge of each 14½×10" rectangle of cotton duck by pressing the edge under twice and machine stitching close to the first fold; press. With right sides together, align the unfinished edges of one rectangle with the top and side edges of the pillow top. Align the unfinished edges of second rectangle with the bottom and sides of the pillow top. The hemmed edges will overlap in the middle. Machine-sew all the way around the pillow. Trim the corners diagonally and turn the pillow cover right side out through the overlapped opening. Arrange the buttons on the border strips as desired and sew them in place with black floss. Insert the pillow form.❤

Designers: Fiddlestix
Photographer: Perry Struse

glittering valentines

Cards measure 4¼×5½" and 6½×5".
Shown *right* and on *page 11*.

MATERIALS
- Cardstock (for card base)
- Decorative paper
- Cardstock or lighter weight paper (for shaker)
- Rubber stamp shaker template (Art Gone Wild X3-1208 or X3-1209)
- Quick drying ink pad
- Scissors and crafts knife
- Clear window plastic
- Double-stick tape
- Foam tape
- Confetti and/or filler such as tiny glass beads, glitter, shells, buttons, etc.
- Ribbon or decorative threads and heart charms

INSTRUCTIONS

From the cardstock, cut one 6½×10" rectangle for a large card base or one 5½×8½" rectangle for a small card base; fold the rectangle in half for the card base. Cut a piece of decorative paper the same size or ¼" to ½" smaller than the folded card; tape it to the card front.

To make a shaker, stamp the template image on the back side of the paper selected for the shaker. To substitute a heart window, trace or draw a heart inside the square window shape. Use a crafts knife to score the cardstock on dotted lines; cut out on solid lines. Using the

measurements of the center rectangle or square created by the dotted lines, cut a piece of decorative paper for the background and a piece of clear plastic for the window.

Place double-stick tape around the sides of the window opening; secure the clear plastic in the window. Place a double layer of foam tape in a square or rectangle around the window opening, overlapping the tape at the corners and being careful not to leave any gaps. Using two layers of tape will allow the confetti to move around inside the window. Fill the area inside the foam tape with confetti or other filler. Firmly press the previously cut background paper, right side down, on the foam tape. Fold in the four flaps; secure with double-stick tape.

Tie ribbon in a bow around shaker or wrap decorative thread with heart charms around the shaker. Attach the assembled shaker to the card front with pieces of foam tape.❤

Designer: Holly Springer
Photographer: Perry Struse

felt heart mat

Mat is 10½" square.
Shown *above* and on *page 12*.

MATERIALS
- Tracing paper
- 16½×18" piece *each* of deep gold and plum crafts felt
- 12" felt square each of cinnamon, cranberry, and sage crafts felt
- Scrap of bright gold crafts felt
- Straight-edge scissors
- Pinking shears or pinking rotary cutter
- Straight pins
- No. 5 black pearl cotton
- No. 24 chenille needle

INSTRUCTIONS

Trace the large heart, small heart, large diamond, small diamond, and triangle shapes, *below,* onto tracing paper; cut out.

Use straight-edged scissors to cut all of the felt pieces, except those where pinking shears or pinking rotary cutter is specified.

From deep gold, use pinking shears to cut one 10½" square for backing. From remaining deep gold, cut two 3½" squares.

From plum, cut one 10" square for background, one large heart, and one small heart.

From bright gold, cut one large diamond.

From cinnamon, cut two 3½" squares and one small heart.

From cranberry, cut two large hearts, one small heart, and four triangles.

From sage, cut one large heart, one small heart, and one small diamond.

Refer to the photograph, *above,* for color placement and to position the pieces. Use the chenille needle and No. 5 black pearl cotton for all embroidery. For the small hearts and small diamond, make the blanket stitches approximately ⅛"-long and ⅛" apart. Slightly increase the stitch length and the distance between the stitches as the felt pieces become larger, making the stitches on the plum background approximately ¼"-long and ¼" apart.

Blanket-stitch a small heart to the center of each large heart, turning over one large cranberry heart for the top left corner. Pin and blanket-stitch the large hearts in place on the 3½" squares.

Position and pin the 3½" squares on the plum background, tilting the squares slightly and keeping them at least 1" from the edges of the background. Blanket-stitch the squares to the background.

Blanket-stitch the small diamond centered on the large diamond. Pin the assembled diamonds centered on the background, overlapping the corners of the 3½" squares. Blanket-stitch a triangle to the outer corner of each 3½" square.

Center and pin the plum background on the deep gold backing; blanket-stitch in place. ❤

Designer: J. Hughes Marte
Photographer: Perry Struse

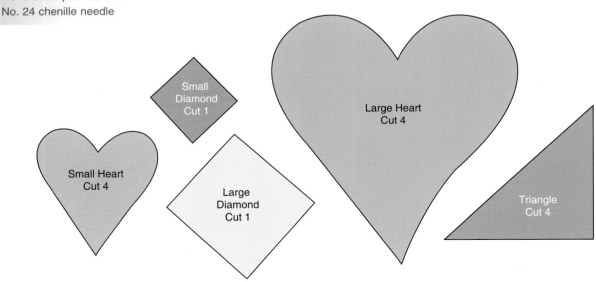

Small Diamond Cut 1

Small Heart Cut 4

Large Diamond Cut 1

Large Heart Cut 4

Triangle Cut 4

blue roses trinket

Shown on *page 13*.

MATERIALS

- 6×5½×½" wood heart with hole
- All-purpose sealer
- Satin varnish
- Paper towels
- Tracing paper
- Sandpaper
- Stylus
- ½"-wide transparent tape
- Brushes: 1" flat, #6, #10 shader, #10/0 liner, ⅜" deerfoot stippler, and sponge brush
- Ribbon

Delta Ceramcoat Colors

- AW Antique White
- GG Gamel Green
- LL Luscious Lemon
- MI Midnight Blue
- PS Purple Smoke
- VG Village Green

INSTRUCTIONS

Use sponge brush to apply one coat of all-purpose sealer to entire heart. Dry. Sand lightly. Use the 1" brush to apply two coats of AW on front of heart, sanding lightly between coats.

Referring to color photo, position ½"-wide tape across top surface of heart, leaving approximately ½" between to create stripes. Use #10 shader to paint the stripes VG.

Trace the pattern at *right*. Use a stylus to transfer the traced design to the heart.

roses

Use a #10 brush to base-coat rose circle with PS. Using #10 brush, shade throat and bottom of rose with floated color using MI.

Using #6 brush, double load brush with PS and AW. Create small scalloped strokes above throat, then comma strokes for the rose petals, working from below the throat of the rose to the base of the rose. (Keep comma strokes well blended and begin outer strokes outside the edge of the rose circle. It's OK to overlap some of the petals.) Use corner of brush to create some AW, then some LL imperfect dots in center of throat.

For the leaves, using a #6 brush, add water to the GG, thinning the paint to an ink consistency. Paint the leaves, sometimes using an "S" stroke and sometimes a comma. Add GG stems and veins with the #10/0 liner.

To paint the outer border, use a #10/0 liner with GG to paint a wavy border around heart, varying the thickness of the line. Pull small stem lines for the leaves away from the wavy line using the 10/0 liner.

Using thinned paint, create small leaves over the stem lines with the #10/0 liner.

With a ⅜" deerfoot stippler, create some "baby's breath" here and there around the roses and leaves, using both AW and LL. Paint back of heart and edges with GG.

For a protective finish, apply two to three coats of satin varnish to entire heart. When the varnish is completely dry, thread the ribbon through the hole at the top. ❤

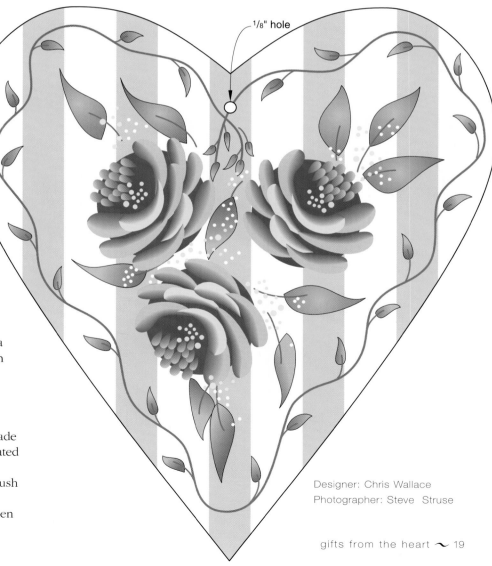

¹⁄₈" hole

Designer: Chris Wallace
Photographer: Steve Struse

Tiny Favor Boxes
start on *page 31.*

anniver

saries
AND
weddings

Sometimes a little help is the best *gift* for a busy bride.
Offer your *creativity* and this assortment of accessories
for her reception, and she'll be *forever* appreciative.

As our marriage brings
new meaning to love
so our love
brings new meaning
to life.

Send wedding or anniversary
party *guests* home with a tangible
memento of the special day, *left.*
Fold a paper doily around
a *message* of thanks,
turn a simple paper tent into
a birdseed container, and
decorate tiny cake boxes.

**Birdseed Tent
starts on *page 31.***

In the sweetness of love
let there be laughter
and in all our tomorrows
the freshness of today
Kimberly and Scott

Capture the *romance* of a favorite couple's wedding day
in one of the picture-perfect *pillows* at *left.* Stitched from a
collection of new "vintage" fabrics and trims, the pillow's focal point
is a large *netting* window. Sewn to the front on three sides,
it becomes a see-through *pocket* for inserting a special
photograph or wedding invitation.

**Wedding
Handkerchief
starts on
*page 32.***

A wedding day or anniversary *celebration* calls for lovely things,
like this delicately embroidered *handkerchief, above.*
Worked in powder blue threads on fine linen, the motif blooms into
a beautiful bride's *bouquet* with satin stitches, French knots,
outline stitches, and pearl accents.

**Picture-Perfect Pillows
start on *page 33.***

Toasting Flutes
start on *page 34*.

Hand-painting and cake decorating techniques put the *icing*
on these eye-catching flutes, *above*. Apply one coat of surface
conditioner to the outside of the *crystal*. When dry, transfer
and paint the pattern. To make the flowers, attach a flower
tip to a decorating bag filled with a special gel *glass* paint.

Surprise the new couple with paper *treasures* as glorious
as their romantic wedding day. Dimensional flowers—in the bride's
chosen colors—*cascade* over this scrapbook entry
and coordinating mint box, *right*. Created with pastel cardstock
and paper punches, the blooms come to *life* when
they're layered and curled.

Scrapbook Entry & Mint Box
start on *page 34*.

Marriage is the most natural state of man, and the state in which you will find solid happiness.
— Benjamin Franklin

Bob and Sandra

Decoupaged Corsage Box
starts on *page 35.*

Presentation is everything. Wrapped, stamped, embossed, and decoupaged, this exceptional papier-mâché box, *left*, almost *outblooms* the gift of roses inside. Let the 6×8-inch oval container hold the corsage until the petals fade, then fill it with *potpourri,* bath soaps, or small trinkets.

Place Card Frames start on *page 37*.

When party guests go to find their seats, *welcome* them with place card favors, *above*. Self-standing and covered in satin, the purchased photo *frames* are ready to whisk into place. Add simple embellishments and a photo or a *handwritten* name.

Painted Candle Collection
starts on *page 29*.

The next time you host a shower or reception, get the tables *glowing* with a candlelight centerpiece.
While plain candles will do, these hand-painted ones serve up a prettier setting—
and work as a *remembrance* to give to the honored couple. The *trio* has been prepared
with a candle-painting medium, then painted with acrylic paints.

painted candle collection

Shown on *page 28*.

MATERIALS

- 3"-diameter white pillar candle
- 3"-diameter white ball candle
- 6"-diameter white three-wick pillar candle
- DecoArt Candle Painting Medium
- Brushes: 1" and #6 flat, #2 liner, #1 liner, #3 round, #10 flat shader

DecoArt Americana Colors

- AV Avocado DA52
- BL Blush Flesh DA110
- CB Country Blue DA41
- HG Hauser Light Green DA131
- MY Moon Yellow DA07
- OR Orchid DA33
- PP Peony Pink DA215
- TW Titanium White DA01
- WI Wisteria DA211

DecoArt Dazzling Metallics

- CG Champagne Gold DA202
- WP White Pearl DA117

INSTRUCTIONS

Use candle-painting medium to clean the candle following manufacturer's instructions. Use the 1" flat brush for all base-coating.

easy diamonds

Mix equal parts candle-painting medium and WP. Base-coat sides of candle using the 1" flat brush.

Referring to the photograph, *opposite,* use the #1 liner to paint CB diamonds about ¼" tall randomly on the candle. Outline each diamond with WI then CG. Use the handle end of the brush to add an OR dot in the center of each CB diamond.

pastel stripes

Mix equal parts candle-painting medium and WI. Base-coat the entire candle using a 1" flat brush. Lightly sponge OR and TW on WI background. Thin CB with a drop or two of water and use the #10 flat shader to paint vertical stripes allowing for 1" of space between them. Use the #1 liner to outline both sides of each stripe with CG.

At the top and bottom of the candle, connect the stripes with wavy lines.

Randomly paint small flowers, using the #1 liner to pull five CB strokes around center. Use the handle end of the brush and MY to dot the center of the flower.

Randomly paint a few leaves around candle. Use the #6 flat brush to paint one-stroke leaves by double-loading the brush with HG and TW. Press bristles down and pull to a point. Use the #1 liner and HG to add a short stroke to the widest part of each leaf for a stem.

rose bouquet

Mix equal parts candle-painting medium and WP. Base-coat sides of candle using the 1" flat brush.

Paint a 1½" band of WI on the top and bottom of the candle. Lightly sponge OR and TW on band.

Use the #10 flat shader to paint vertical stripes of CB thinned with a drop or two of water. Allow for 1" of space between stripes.

Continued

easy diamonds

pastel stripes

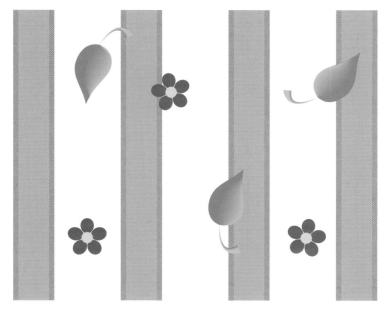

painted candle collection

Use the #1 liner to outline both sides of each stripe with CG.

Finish bands by creating a wavy horizontal band of CG on the top and bottom of each band referring to the photo on *page 28*.

Use the #6 flat brush to create a cluster of leaves between the two bands and slightly overlapping. To make large leaves, double-load brush with HG and TW. Press bristles down and pull to a point, then repeat on the other side of the stroke, bringing the two points together. Add some darker leaves with AV and HG to add depth and fullness to the cluster. Once satisfied with the shape, use the #1 liner to pull short blades of grass and vines on the outer perimeter of the cluster. Use the same brush to paint tiny leaves on the vines.

To create large pink flowers, double-load the #6 flat brush with OR and PP. Create a "c" stroke for the back of the bud with the PP side of the brush kept at the base of the flower. Repeat the stroke in the opposite direction for the front of the bud, beginning and ending at the other stroke. Make four small circles around the base of the bud for petals by holding the PP side of the brush stationary and pivoting the OR side halfway around per photo. Use the #1 liner to add short white highlights on the OR side of the bud and petals.

Use the #3 round to make BL flowers. Double-load brush with TW and BL. Press brush down and pull to a point several times around a central point. Use the #1 liner to paint MY flower center.

To make little flowers, use the #1 liner to pull five CB strokes around center. Use the handle end of the brush and MY to dot the center of the flower.

Use TW on the handle end of the brush to add little clusters of dots per photo.

Helpful Hint: *Save the artwork on your large candles by letting the candles burn down 1½" to 2" around wicks. Place a tea light in each cavity.*♥

Designer: Margaret Goss
Photographer: Perry Struse

rose bouquet

tiny favor boxes

Square box measures 2¼". Rectangle box measures 3½×2¼×1½". Doily envelope measures 5¾" square. Birdseed tent measures 3" tall. Shown on *pages 20–21*.

MATERIALS

For all containers
- Colorbox gold pigment ink
- Stampendous gold embossing powder
- Heat source, such as embossing heat tool, toaster, or iron

For the square box
- Stampendous precut square box
- Stamps: PSX Rose #B2233 and River City Rubber Works Thank You #1233-D
- 1½"-wide sheer ribbon
- 1¼×2½" rectangle of white cardstock
- Silk flowers
- Gold cord

For the rectangle box
- Stampendous precut rectangle box
- PSX Stamps: Rose #B2233, Love and Marriage #C3028, and 3 Doves #G3001
- 1½"-wide sheer ribbon
- Silk leaves and berries

For the birdseed tent
- 3×7½" rectangle of decorative cardstock
- Ruler and crafts knife
- 7½" length of 1⅜"-wide ribbon
- Double-stick tape
- Small resealable bag
- Birdseed
- 2⅜×1¾" rectangle of white cardstock
- 2⅝×2" rectangle of gold cardstock
- Marriage saying stamp
- Clay or silk flowers
- Glue gun and hotmelt adhesive

For the doily envelope
- 10" square paper doily
- 1 sheet of decorative paper, white typing paper, and vellum
- Double-stick tape
- Stamp Your Art Out scalloped gift envelope template
- 1⅜"-wide white grosgrain ribbon

- 1½"-wide sheer ribbon
- 2" white paper heart
- PSX Stamps: Rose #B2233, Love and Marriage #C3028, and 3 Doves #G3001
- Self-adhesive Velcro circle

INSTRUCTIONS

To emboss, stamp the selected images on the paper or ribbon with pigment ink. Immediately sprinkle with gold embossing powder. Tilt the paper or ribbon up on edge and tap off the excess powder. Hold the paper or ribbon near a heat source until the powder melts, creating a shiny, raised image.

square box

Emboss roses on the unassembled box. Assemble the box.

For the gift tag, fold the cardstock rectangle in half. Emboss a single rose on the front of the gift tag and "Thank You" inside. Tie the ribbon in a bow around the box. Thread gold cord through a top corner of the tag; knot cord around the center of the ribbon bow. Slip silk flowers inside the ribbon knot.

doily envelope

From the decorative paper, cut a 9¼" square; tape the decorative paper centered on the wrong side of doily. Use the computer to write a special message to the guests and print it on white typing paper. Trim the paper into a 5½" square with the message at the top; leave room at the bottom for the envelope. Turn the decorative paper so a corner is the top; tape the message paper centered on the decorative paper. Trace the scalloped gift envelope onto vellum; cut out.

Continued

tiny favor boxes

Fold the corners in to form a small envelope; tape to secure the edges. Tape small envelope on the message paper below the text. Fold in the corners of the doily just beyond the message paper in this order; sides, bottom, and top.

Emboss doves on the grosgrain ribbon and a rose and "Love and Marriage" on the white heart. Center and tape the heart to the embossed ribbon. Layer sheer ribbon atop. Wrap the layered ribbons around the envelope; secure the ends at the back with a Velcro circle.

birdseed tent
Score the decorative cardstock 3", 6", and 7" from one short edge; fold on the score lines, creating a tent shape with a ½"-wide end tab. Tape the ribbon on the tent ¼" from the right edge. Tape a small bag of birdseed inside the tent. Place double-stick tape on the right side of the end tab; press the opposite edge onto tape.

Emboss the marriage saying on the 2⅜×1¾" rectangle of white cardstock. Use double-stick tape to layer the saying on the gold cardstock and

then on the tent front. Glue a flower on the front.

rectangle box
Emboss "Love and Marriage" and roses on the lid of the unassembled box and doves on the sides. Assemble the box. Hot glue leaves and berries to the lid. ♥

Designer: Suzanne State
Photographer: Perry Struse

---

wedding handkerchief

Shown on *page 23*.

MATERIALS
- Purchased 10½" square linen handkerchief
- Cotton embroidery floss
- Tracing paper
- Erasable marker
- Needle
- Embroidery hoop
- 2.5mm round pearls

INSTRUCTIONS
Trace the pattern, *right*. Tape it on a light box or a brightly lit window. Place the handkerchief over the tracing and use the erasable marker to trace it onto the handkerchief. Following the stitching guide, stitch the stems first, then the leaves and

flowers. Stitch the French knots last. Attach the pearls using one strand of floss as indicated on the pattern. ♥

Designer: Alice Okon
Photographer: Scott Little

Anchor		DMC
STEM STITCH		
159	╱	775 Baby blue (2X)
SATIN STITCH		
159	◗	775 Baby blue (1X)
FRENCH KNOT		
159	○	775 Baby blue (1X)
ATTACHMENTS		
	○	2.5mm white round pearls

picture-perfect pillows

Shown on *pages 22–23*.

MATERIALS
- 1—12×16" pillow
- 5×7" piece of off-white tulle
- Fabric glue
- Assorted fabric flowers, bead tassels, ribbons, and other trims

For the ivory pillow
- ¾ yard of 4"-wide ivory satin fringe
- 1¾ yards of 6"-wide ecru rayon fringe
- 1¾ yards ½"-wide ecru crochet-style lace
- ½ yard of 2"-wide ecru cotton lace
- ½ yard of 2" wide ecru pregathered silk lace with scalloped edge
- ½ yard of ⅝" wide ecru scalloped-edge lace
- 4×6" photo

For the print pillow
- ¾ yard of 6"-wide ivory rayon fringe
- 1¼ yards of lace fringe
- ½ yard of drapery trim in pillow colors

INSTRUCTIONS
Make a "ledge" around the pillow to attach the fringe and trims by carefully stitching around the pillow ½" from the edge. If there is a pillow form inside the pillow, adjust it just enough to avoid stitching it.

For the print pillow, sew or use glue to secure the 6" ivory rayon fringe, then the lace fringe to the ledge at each end.

For the ivory pillow, secure the satin fringe to the ledge at each end of the pillow. Secure the 6" rayon fringe, then the ½"-wide crocheted lace all the way around.

Center the tulle on the pillow and glue three edges to the top of the pillow, leaving the one edge open.

For the print pillow, secure the edge of the remaining fringe lace and the drapery fabric trim to the three secured edges of the tulle.

For the ivory pillow, secure the 2"-wide cotton lace around the secured edges of the tulle. Secure the pregathered silk lace close to the outer edge of the cotton lace. Then secure the ⅝"-wide scalloped-edge lace over the seam where the two wide laces meet. Sew or glue ¾" ribbon, lace, or gimp over top edges of 2"-wide cotton lace.

Add desired trims to the corner of the photo pocket. Slide your favorite 4×6" photo into the tulle pocket. ♥

Designer: Carole Cree
Photographer: Scott Little

toasting flutes

Glasses are 9¾" tall. Shown on *page 24*.

MATERIALS
- Tracing paper
- Transfer paper
- Long-stemmed champagne glasses
- Lint-free towel
- Delta PermEnamel Surface Conditioner
- Parchment cake decorating bag
- Cake decorating standard coupler
- Small 5-petal flower cake decorating tip (such as Wilton #129, 224, 190, or 140)
- Brushes: #4 shader, #1 liner

Delta Air-Dry PermEnamel Paints
- HG Hunter Green 45032
- UW Ultra White 45029

Delta PermEnamel Textured
Gel Glass Paint
- PL Pearl 45732

Delta PermEnamel Accent Liner
- GD Gold 45811

INSTRUCTIONS

prepare the glasses
Trace the pattern, *page 34,* onto tracing paper; cut out, leaving a ¼" margin around the design.

Wash the glasses in warm soapy water; rinse thoroughly and dry with a lint-free towel. Apply one coat of

Continued

toasting flutes

the surface conditioner to the outside surface of the glass; let the conditioner dry. Avoid touching the prepared surface of the glasses. Begin painting within 4 hours; reapplying the surface conditioner if longer.

paint the glasses

Refer to the photograph, *page 33,* and the pattern as guides for shading and details. For solid coverage, apply two even, thin coats when base-coating; let paint dry between coats. Brushes can be rinsed between colors but must be dried before dipping into the next color; never dilute the paints with water.

Transfer the main pattern lines onto one glass. Do not transfer the details, as you'll base-coat over them. Reverse the pattern and transfer to the second glass.

Mix 4 parts UW with 1 part HG. Use this mixture and the #4 shader to base-coat the solid shaped areas on the glasses. When the base coat is dry, use the #4 shader to float HG shading along the top edge of the painted shapes. Use HG and the #1 liner brush to base-coat the leaves and add the stems.

add the texture

To make flowers, attach the flower tip to the decorating bag. First place the large part of the coupler down into the bag. Then put the flower tip on the coupler, and screw the small part of the coupler over the tip and bag. Squeeze about one-third to half of the texture gel into the bag.

Lay the glass, paint side up, on a towel and bunch the towel up around the glass to keep it from rolling. Hold the bag straight up and down over the glass. Touch the point of the flower tip on the glass; squeeze the bag until the gel is touching the surface. While still squeezing, rotate

your wrist a half turn. Stop squeezing and lift the bag off of the glass, creating a flower with a point. Let the flowers dry for a couple hours and very lightly tap the points with your finger to flatten. If the gel sticks to your finger, let the flowers set a little longer.

Use the gold accent liner to make the lines of dots around the design and at the center of the flowers.

Let the glasses dry 10 days before using or hand-washing them. ♥

Designer: Chris Thornton
Photographer: Perry Struse

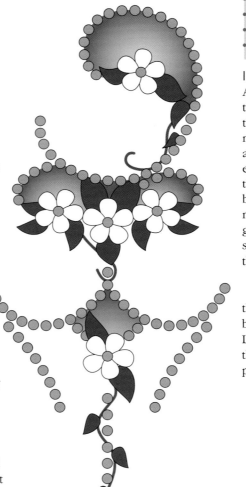

scrapbook entry & mint box

Shown on *pages 24–25.*

MATERIALS

- 8½×11" archival-quality photo album page
- Lace border stickers
- Beige, blue, pale blue, lavender, pale peach, and green papers
- Scallop-edge scissors
- Fine-tip metallic gold marking pen
- Color copy of wedding photo
- Decorative paper punches: Jumbo Craft Punch 1"-wide daisy, All Night Media ⅝"-wide flower, and 1"-wide four-hearts
- Assorted seed beads
- Acid-free glue
- Purchased small bag
- 8" length of 1½"-wide sheer ribbon

INSTRUCTIONS

Adhere lace border stickers around the edges of the album page. Use the gold marking pen to write a message on the beige paper; trim around the message with the scallop-edge scissors. Trim the photo around the wedding couple, eliminating the background. Position the photo and message paper on the page as desired; glue in place. Adhere narrow lace stickers around the straight edges of the photo.

For each large dimensional flower, use the 1"-wide daisy punch to punch three or four flowers from the light blue, lavender, or pale peach paper. Layer the three or four flowers on the album page. When you are pleased with the arrangement, glue

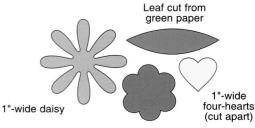

Leaf cut from green paper

1"-wide daisy

1"-wide four-hearts (cut apart)

⅝"-wide flower

the layers together and curl the petals up slightly. Repeat to make as many large flowers as desired.

For each small dimensional flower, use the ⅝"-wide flower paper to punch two flowers from the blue, light blue, lavender, or pale peach paper. Layer the small flowers on the page. Glue the flowers in place, curling the top layer of petals up slightly. Repeat to make as many flowers as desired.

Use the four-heart punch to punch hearts from a variety of paper colors. Glue the small hearts around the flowers to fill in any gaps. Cut leaves from the green paper. Glue the leaves to the page, slipping one end under the flowers.

When the glue is dry, glue one to three seed beads at the center of the small flowers and approximately 10 beads at the center of the large flowers.

Use the gold marking pen to shade several of the scallops around the message paper. Referring to the photos, *left,* for ideas, use the marking pen to embellish the bottom corners of the photo and to extend the flower lines. Add the couple's name along the bottom of the photo.

For the gift bag, make flowers as for the album page, positioning a single large flower on the flap and a group of flowers on the center front of the bag. Cut a 2¾×1½" gift tag and punch a daisy in one half.

To attach the tag, wrap the sheer ribbon around the handle and through the daisy punch; tie a knot. ❤

Designer: Beverly Rivers
Photographer: Perry Struse

decoupaged corsage box

Box measures 6×8". Shown on *page 26.*

MATERIALS
- Rose rubber stamp
- Pigment ink stamp pad
- Gold embossing powder
- Heat source, such as embossing heat tool, toaster, or iron
- White, gold, and mauve cardstock
- Bright-colored marking pens
- 6×8" oval papier-mâché box
- Rose wrapping paper
- Tape measure
- Decoupage medium
- Sponge brush
- ½"-wide double-stick tape
- ⅝"-wide ribbon (we used 1¼ yards)
- Cherub charm
- Needle and thread

INSTRUCTIONS
Stamp roses on the white cardstock with pigment ink. Immediately sprinkle with gold embossing powder. Tilt the cardstock up on edge and tap off the excess powder. Hold the cardstock near a heat source until the powder melts, creating a shiny, raised image. Use marking pens to color the roses.

Tear the white cardstock into an oval around the embossed roses; our oval measures 2¾×5". Layer the white oval on the gold cardstock and tear a slightly larger oval from the gold. Set ovals aside.

Place the box lid, top down, on the wrong side of the wrapping paper. Use a pencil to trace around the lid. Cut out the shape, adding a ½" margin for tabs. Trace the box lid a second time; cut out the shape for the inside of lid, adding a ¼" margin. Use a tape measure to determine the circumference of the lid; add ½" for overlap. Measure the height of the lid; multiply by 2. Use these measurements to cut a strip of wrapping paper for the sides of the lid.

Place the box base on the mauve cardstock. Trace around the base, cut out the shape for the inside of the base, adding a ¼" margin. Use a tape measure to find the circumference of the base; add ½" for overlap. Measure the height of the base; add 1" for the top tabs. Use these measurements to cut a piece of wrapping paper for the base sides. Find the circumference inside the base; add ½" for overlap. Measure the height inside the base; subtract ¼". Use these measurements to cut a piece of mauve cardstock for the inside of base.

Lay the wrapping paper shape for the top of lid, right side down, on a covered work surface. Use a sponge

Continued

decoupaged corsage box

brush to apply an even coat of decoupage medium to the paper shape, beginning at the center and working out to the edges. Center the piece of paper on the lid, smoothing from the center out. Fold the margins down onto the lid sides, using scissors to clip a tab every 1". Apply decoupage medium to the wrong side of the wrapping paper shape for the inside of the lid. Center the paper inside the lid, smoothing from the center out and working the margins onto the sides.

For the lid sides, apply decoupage medium to the wrapping paper strip and press the strip onto the lid sides. Fold the strip around the bottom edge and inside the lid, clipping the paper as needed.

Apply decoupage medium to the wrapping paper for the box base sides. Press the paper onto the base sides, keeping the bottom edge even with the bottom of the box. Fold the margins into the box at the top, clipping tabs as needed. Apply decoupage medium to the mauve cardstock shape for inside of base. Center the cardstock inside the lid, smoothing from the center out and working the margins onto the sides. Apply decoupage medium to the mauve cardstock for the sides inside the base and press in place.

Use decoupage medium to secure the ovals to the top of the lid. Apply two coats of decoupage medium to all surfaces of the lid and base, letting dry between coats.

Beginning and ending at the mauve cardstock inside the box base, run double-stick tape down the sides and across the bottom of the base. Press ribbon onto the tape. Beginning and ending inside the box lid, run double-stick tape down the sides and across the top of the lid. Tie a bow in the center of the remaining ribbon. Press the ribbon onto the tape, positioning the bow at the center of the box. Sew the charm to the knot in the bow. ♥

Designer: Roberta Royse
Photographer: Perry Struse

Glue one cardboard surface to the frame front and one cardboard surface to the frame back. Dab glue on the wire ends and stick the wire into the center top of the bell.

beaded frame
Pour white beads onto a paper plate. Use a brush to apply a thin, even coat of glue to the front of the frame. Immediately dip the glued surface into the plate of beads.

trimmed frame
Wrap the trim or ribbon lengths around the bottom corners of the frame and glue the ends to the frame back. ♥

Designer: Carrie Topp
Photographer: Marcia Cameron

place card frames

Place cards measure 4×3".
Shown on *page 27*.

MATERIALS
- Purchased 4×3" frames with oval openings
- Assorted embellishments: green silk ribbon and purchased rosebud; or 2½" wedding bell, 12" length of 28-gauge brass wire, and three pearl beads; or no-hole white glass beads, small foam brush, and paper plate; or short lengths of ⅜"-wide trim or ribbon
- Crafts glue
- Parchment paper
- Fine-tip gold marking pen

INSTRUCTIONS
Embellish the frames as described below. Let the glue dry. Cut pieces of parchment paper to fit in the oval frame openings. Personalize the parchment paper with the gold marking pen; slip the papers into the frames.

rose frame
Wrap green silk ribbon around the rosebud stem, leaving 4 to 5" tails. Glue the rosebud to the front of the frame.

bell frame
Thread the pearl beads onto the brass wire. Shape the wire, separating the beads and bringing the wire ends together. Open the bell around one edge of the frame.

Star Picture Frame
starts on *page 50*.

"Oohs" and *coos* greet this
precious collection of gifts
for the new arrival! Ideas from
crochet and embroidery to
scrapbooking, quilting, and
painting fill these pages,
starting with the *dreamy*
album cover and painted wood
photo frame, *right,* and the
sentimental ornament, *above.*
Give them at showers,
on the baby's *birth* date,
and in the toddler years ahead.

WELCOMING THE
new
arrival

Above: **Personalized Ornament**
starts on *page 56*.

**Scrapbook Album
starts on *page 52*.**

Shhh... Sign
starts on *page 52.*

Sweet *dreams,* little one. This sleepytime sign with its softly chiseled surface
and edging, *above,* starts as a *slate* base (available at crafts stores). Base-coated
in beige, the piece is then dry-brushed in a subtle *rainbow* of colors. The moon
and lettering are hand-painted, too.

No time to *crochet* an entire blanket? Pick a cozy purchased one and add
your own heirloom edging. *Lacy* and *lovely,* this 2-inch-wide trim, *right,* makes the
most of soft, washable yarn and a few basic stitches—single crochet,
double crochet, and an occasional triple.

Lacy Blanket Edging
starts on *page 54*.

Left to right: **Diaper Cake** starts on *page 54.*

Personalized Baby Accessories start on *page 56.*

Here's a new version of a baby shower *favorite.* Serving as centerpiece and gift, the tiered *"cake"* is created by rolling cloth diapers into coils and basting them together around a plastic-foam center. Slip toys, clothing, and other *newborn* supplies between the diaper folds and rolls.

Rows of hearts here, *curlicues* and dots there, everywhere, easy touches with *pastel* paint pens. In just a bit of time, you can change plastic *accessories* and Christmas baubles into treasures for the newborn and mother. Be sure to check your paint pens for washing care. Some are dishwasher safe, while others require hand-washing.

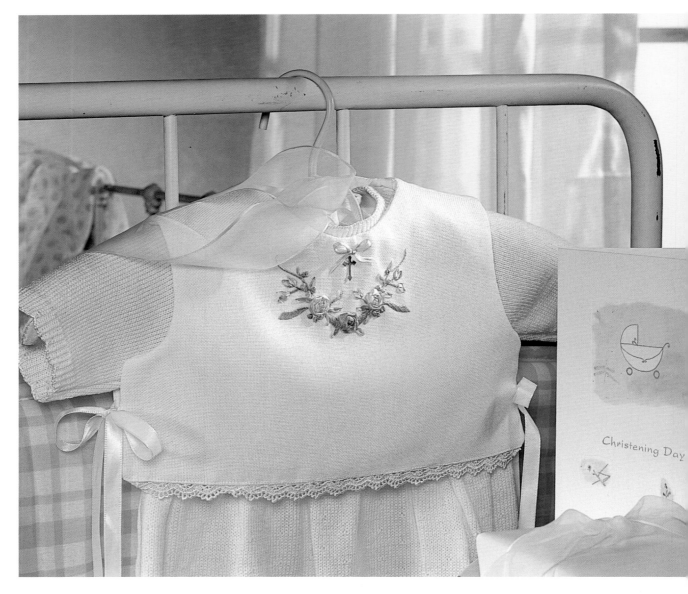

When only something as *sweet* and lovely as your newborn will do,
embellish it in *rosebuds*. Here, a delicate garland of ribbon roses and
pastel threads rises to the *neckline* of a purchased bodice-style tabard, *above*.
The design adapts with ease to other baby garments, too.

**Ribbon Embroidered
Christening Overlay
starts on *page 57*.**

Sew a child's drawing into a *welcoming* wardrobe addition for a new arrival.
This bibbed overall and brimmed bonnet duo, *right*, feature a little one's *artwork,*
or you can personalize the fashions with *postcard* prints or photos.
It's done in a breeze with iron-on transfer paper.

Transfer-Embellished Children's Clothing starts on *page 58*.

A supply bag this *versatile* grows right along with the new arrival. Stitched with chenille pockets and topped by a trio of *redwork* robins, the bag serves as storage for lotions, wash cloths, and binkies at first. Later, its sturdy nature is practical for holding little books, shoes, and coloring *supplies.* Fold it into thirds, and it buttons for a handy carryall.

Redwork Hanging Supply Bag starts on *page 60.*

**I Spy Quilt
starts on *page 49*.**

What does baby *spy?* A pool of purple turtles? A rocket
to the moon? Dozens of whimsical patches—each with a *story*
to tell—fill this quilt with mystery and fun. Cut each *hexagon* from
a separate fabric or use pairs for a matching game.

i spy quilt

Finished quilt top: 28×36".
Shown on *page 48*.

MATERIALS

- 82—5" squares of assorted novelty prints for blocks (For an I Spy quilt use 82 different prints. For a Match-It quilt use 41 different prints; repeat each once.)
- 1 yard of bright yellow print for background
- 1 yard of backing fabric
- 34×42" of quilt batting

Quantities specified are for 44/45" wide, 100% cotton fabrics. All measurements include a ⅜" seam allowance.

INSTRUCTIONS

cut the fabrics

To make the best use of your fabrics cut the pieces in the order that follows. Cut all strips across the width of the fabric.

Use pattern pieces A and B, *page 50,* to make plastic templates to cut the fabric pieces. Patterns A and B can be cut with the Come Quilt With Me 3½"-Diameter Hexagon template set.

These border strip measurements are mathematically correct. You may wish to add extra length to the border strips when cutting to allow for possible sewing differences.

From yellow print, cut:
- 2—2×28½" border strips
- 4—2×42" binding strips
- 12 of hexagon Pattern A
- 186 of triangle Pattern B

From assorted novelty prints, cut:
- 82 of hexagon Pattern A

assemble the rows

Sew a triangle to the upper right side of each novelty print hexagon. Sew a second triangle to the lower left side, opposite the first one to

Diagram 1
Unit 1

Diagram 2
Unit 2

make 82 of Unit 1 (see Diagram 1). Press the seam allowances toward the triangles.

Sew a triangle to the upper right side of each yellow background hexagon to make 12 of Unit 2 (see Diagram 2). Press the seam allowances toward the triangles.

Lay out seven Unit 1 pieces in a row; add a Unit 2 piece to each end. Sew together to make Row 1 (see Diagram 3). Press the seam allowances in one direction. Repeat to make a total of six of Row 1.

Lay out eight Unit 1 pieces in a row; add a yellow triangle to each end. Sew together to make Row 2 (see Diagram 4). Press the seam allowances in one direction. Repeat to make a total of five of Row 2.

assemble the quilt center

Referring to the photograph for placement, lay out the pieced rows, alternating Row 1 and Row 2. Sew the rows together. Press the seam allowances in one direction.

Trim off the extra fabric at the sides, keeping a ¼" seam allowance (see Diagram 5).

add the border

Sew a yellow print 2×28½" border strip to the top and bottom edges of the pieced quilt center. Press the seam allowances toward the borders.

complete the quilt

Layer the quilt top, batting, and backing. Machine quilt in the ditch around all blocks, continuing the quilting line into the borders. Trim the batting and backing even with the quilt top.

Sew the yellow print 2×42" strips together with diagonal seams to form one long binding strip. Trim the excess fabric, leaving ¼" seam allowances. Press the seam allowances open. With the wrong sides together, fold the binding strip in half lengthwise and press. Beginning in the center of one long side of the quilt, place the binding strip against the right side of the quilt top, aligning the binding strip's raw edge with the quilt top's raw edge. Fold over the beginning of the binding strip about ½". Sew around the quilt, mitering corners. Press the fold of the binding to the wrong side and hand-stitch along the seam line.♥

Designer: Pat Yamin
Photographer: Marcia Cameron

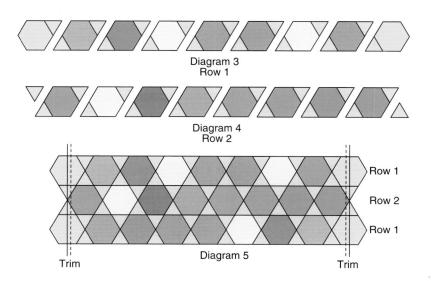

Diagram 3
Row 1

Diagram 4
Row 2

Row 1
Row 2
Row 1

Trim   Diagram 5   Trim

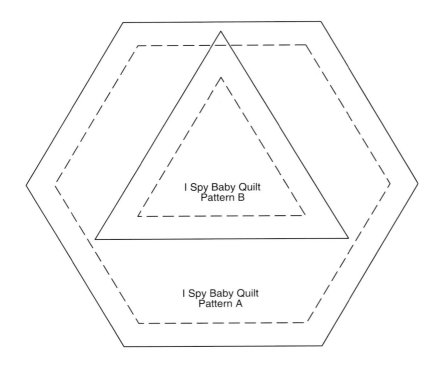

I Spy Baby Quilt
Pattern B

I Spy Baby Quilt
Pattern A

star picture frame

Frame measures 9½×10", with a 3¼×2½"
photo opening. Shown on *page 38*.

MATERIALS
- Tracing paper
- Graphite or transfer paper
- 1×10×11" piece of pine
- ¼×3×4" piece of Baltic birch plywood
- Scrollsaw
- Medium- and fine-grit sandpaper
- Tack cloth
- Wood sealer
- Toothpicks
- Fine-tip permanent black marking pen,
  such as Pigma .001
- 5-minute epoxy
- Blair Satin Tole spray varnish
- Sawtooth hanger
- Photo and medium-weight cardboard
- Brushes: ¾" wash, ½" wash, #2 shader,
  #4 shader, #8 shader, #12 shader,
  18/0 script liner, ½" stippler, and
  ⅜" stippler

DecoArt Americana Colors
- AR Antique Rose DA156
- BS Burnt Sienna DA63
- BU Burnt Umber DA64
- BK Buttermilk DA3
- GB French Gray Blue DA98
- HF Hi-Lite Flesh DA24
- HB Honey Brown DA163
- LB Lamp Black DA67
- LF Light French Blue DA185
- MF Medium Flesh DA102
- MC Milk Chocolate DA174
- MY Moon Yellow DA7
- RA Raspberry DA28
- TF Taffy Cream DA5
- UB Uniform Blue 86
- WR Winter Blue DA190

INSTRUCTIONS

cut the wood

On tracing paper, complete the star/
angel and hand patterns, *opposite*. Use
graphite paper to transfer the outline
of the star/angel onto the 1" pine.
Transfer one of each hand onto the ¼"
Baltic birch plywood. Cut out the shapes
with a scrollsaw, removing the rectangle
from the center of the star for photo
opening. Dado the backside of the
opening to inset the photo.

Sand all surfaces of the pieces with
medium- and then fine-grit sandpaper.
Remove the sanding dust with a tack
cloth. Apply wood sealer to all
surfaces, and let the sealer dry. Sand
again with fine-grit sandpaper, and
wipe clean with a tack cloth.

paint the pieces
Base-coat with the wash brush that
best fits the area. Use shader brushes
to float shading. Apply details with
the script liner brush. Dry-brush on
highlights with the ½" stippler. Use
the tip of a toothpick to make dots.
Avoid painting areas where they'll be
joined later, as epoxy does not bond
permanently to painted surfaces.

Transfer the main design lines
onto the star/angel with graphite
paper. Don't transfer the details yet,
you'll base-coat over them. Base-coat
only the front and side surfaces,
continuing the colors around the
edges of the pieces.

Base-coat the wings BK. Base-coat
the hands and face MF and the hair
MC. Use MY to base-coat the star.
Base-coat the sleeves LF.

When the paint is completely dry,
sand the pieces with a paper grocery
sack to remove the wood grain raised
by the paint. Remove the sanding
dust with a tack cloth. Add the details
to the front of the star/angel.

Use BS to shade the face next to
the hair and the outer edges of the
hands. Dry-brush HF highlights on the
hands. Dry-brush the cheeks with AR.
Dot the eyes with LB. When the eyes
are dry, add a tiny BK dot to each eye
and cheek. Make BU squiggly lines
on the hair.

For the plaid wings, make fine RA
lines. Shade the sleeves next to the
star with UB. Make fine RA lines on
the sleeves and add RA dots between
the lines. Dry-brush highlights on the
sleeves with WR.

Use the ⅜" stippler to randomly
stipple BK flower centers on the star.
Thin HB with water to ink consistency,
and paint the flower petals on the
star around the flower centers. Make

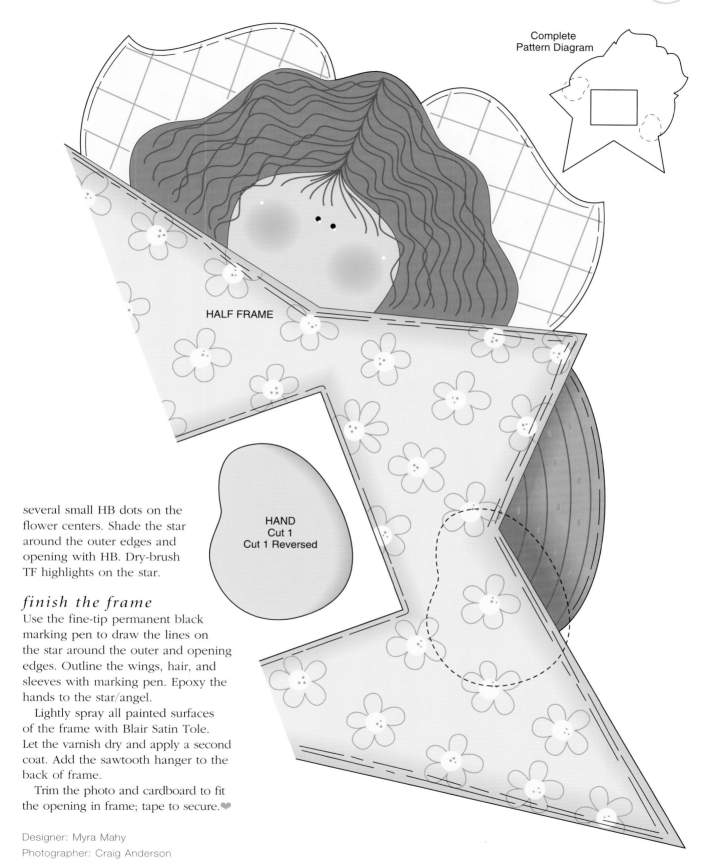

Complete
Pattern Diagram

HALF FRAME

HAND
Cut 1
Cut 1 Reversed

several small HB dots on the
flower centers. Shade the star
around the outer edges and
opening with HB. Dry-brush
TF highlights on the star.

finish the frame

Use the fine-tip permanent black
marking pen to draw the lines on
the star around the outer and opening
edges. Outline the wings, hair, and
sleeves with marking pen. Epoxy the
hands to the star/angel.

Lightly spray all painted surfaces
of the frame with Blair Satin Tole.
Let the varnish dry and apply a second
coat. Add the sawtooth hanger to the
back of frame.

Trim the photo and cardboard to fit
the opening in frame; tape to secure. ♥

Designer: Myra Mahy
Photographer: Craig Anderson

scrapbook album

Album measures 10×11½".
Shown *above* and on *page 39.*

MATERIALS
- Post-bound scrapbook with 8½×11" pages
- 2 varieties of embossed white paper
- Blue and yellow mulberry paper
- Blue paper
- Yellow star-motif background paper
- Double-stick tape
- 1⅛"-tall letter stencil
- Fine-tip permanent black marking pen
- 3—¾" wooden stars
- Drill
- Yellow acrylic paint
- Paintbrush
- Yellow embroidery floss
- 18" of ½"-wide sheer blue ribbon
- Acid-free glue

INSTRUCTIONS
Unscrew post in album and take completely apart. Use blue mulberry paper and double-stick tape to cover the front and back covers. Put the album back together.

To make layered letter blocks, cut a total of four 1¾" squares from the embossed white papers. From the blue paper, cut four squares about ⅛" larger than the white squares. From the yellow mulberry paper, tear four 2¾" squares. Use double-stick tape to attach the layers. Use the letter stencil and a fine-tip black marking pen to trace "BABY" onto the blue paper; cut out the letters just beyond the traced lines. Adhere the letters to the layered blocks.

Drill a small hole through one point of each star. Paint the wooden stars yellow; let the paint dry. From yellow embroidery floss, cut three lengths of floss varying in length from 6 to 8". Insert a length of thread through the hole in each star; bring ends of thread together.

From embossed white paper, cut a 6" tall crescent moon. Use a black marking pen to outline the moon just inside the cut edges. To attach the wooden stars, cut a small hole in the moon, referring to the photo, *above,* for placement. Insert the

thread ends through the hole from front to back; secure ends to the back of moon with double-stick tape. Wrap the sheer ribbon around the white moon and tie in a bow, covering the hole; secure with tape. Adhere the white moon to yellow mulberry paper with tape; tear the yellow paper about ½" beyond the yellow moon.

Adhere the letter blocks and the moon to the front of the album with double-stick tape. Cut small stars from star-motif paper; glue randomly to the album cover. ♥

Designer: Roberta Royse
Photographer: Craig Anderson

shhh…sign

Sign measures 8×5¼". Shown on *page 40.*

MATERIALS
- Tracing paper
- Cape Cod Cooperage small oval slate
- Acrylic spray sealer
- Sea sponge
- Plastic bag (optional)
- Graphite or transfer paper
- Toothpicks
- Krylon 1311 matte spray
- 24" length of 2"-wide rainbow silk ribbon
- Brushes: 1" flat, ½" filbert comb, #4 flat, #0 liner

Plaid FolkArt Colors
- CA Camel 953
- LG Light Gray 424
- MK Milkshake 704
- SN Sunflower 432
- SH Sweetheart Pink 955
- TP Tapioca 903
- WB Whipped Berry 759

Plaid FolkArt Artists' Pigments
- DP Dioxazine Purple 463
- TW Titanium White 480

INSTRUCTIONS
Trace the pattern, *right,* onto tracing paper. Remove the leather strap and

STEP 1

STEP 2

wash the slate in warm water, rinse and dry. Spray or brush on acrylic sealer; let dry.

Use the 1" flat brush to base-coat all surfaces of the slate MK. While the base-coat is still wet, use the sea sponge to apply first CA and then TP to the front surface of the slate as shown in Step 1. There is no need to clean the sponge between colors. Immediately bunch up a plastic bag or use the sea sponge to lightly sponge MK over the wet surface, melding together the colors. Let the paint dry.

Using a ½" filbert comb, dry-brush WB in a crisscross manner over the front surface of the sign; leaving a 2" border of the base-coat finish. Repeat with SH and LG as shown in Step 2, cleaning and drying the brush before using a new color. It is not necessary for the paint to dry between colors.

When the paint is completely dry, transfer the design onto the slate with graphite paper. Use TW to paint "Shhh" with the #4 flat brush. Add the fine lines at the end of the

letters with the liner. For the periods, dip the handle end of a paintbrush in TW and make large dots. Dilute DP with water to ink consistency, and use the liner to paint "... little one's sleeping". Use SN to paint the moon with the #4 flat brush and the stars with the liner. Add the tiny TW dots to the letters, moon, and stars with the tip of a toothpick.

Lightly spray all painted surfaces of the slate with Krylon 1311 matte spray. Insert the ribbon ends through the slate from back to front, knot to form hanging loop. ♥

Designer: Carrie Topp
Photographer: Craig Anderson

lacy blanket edging

The finished blanket is 34×44". Shown *above* and on *page 41*.

MATERIALS
- 3—1.75-oz. balls of Bluette (425) J. & P. Coats Luster Sheen, 100% acrylic yarn
- Size D/3 (3.25 mm) aluminum crochet hook
- Purchased 30×40"receiving blanket
- Sewing needle and matching thread

Gauge
Foundation row plus rows 1 and 2 = 2" wide and 2" long.

Crochet Abbreviations
ch chain
dc double crochet
trc treble crochet
sk skip
sp space
sc single crochet
sl st slip stitch

INSTRUCTIONS

foundation
Ch 9. 2 dc in 8th ch from hook, 2 dc in next ch; turn. Ch 3 (counts as dc), dc in same dc as beginning ch-3; 2

dc in each of the next 3 dc, ch 2, sk 2 ch, trc in next ch; turn.

trim pattern
Row 1: Ch 5 (counts as dc, ch 2); sk ch-2 sp, 2 dc. In each of the next 2 dc, (ch 2, sk 2 dc, dc in next dc) twice; turn.

Row 2: Ch 5 (counts as dc, ch 2); sk ch-2 sp, dc in next dc, ch 2, sk ch-2 sp, 2 dc in each of next 4 dc, ch 2, sk 2 ch, trc in next ch; turn.

Rep rows 1 and 2 for 120 times more. Using needle and sewing thread, sew trim to blanket inside of the border, overlapping the last edge over first edge by one pattern. After you are certain that the trim will fit, fasten off.

Join yarn with a sl st in any center diamond at lower edge. Ch 1, in same sp work (4 sc, ch 3, 4 sc); * ch 5, (4 sc, ch 3, 4 sc) in next center diamond; rep from * around entire edge. At end, join with a sl st in beginning sc and fasten off. ♥

Designer: Ann E. Smith
Photographer: Marcia Cameron

diaper cake

Diaper cake measures approximately 15" tall. Shown *opposite* and on *page 42*.

MATERIALS
- 3—1½" tall plastic-foam 6"-diameter circles
- Crafts glue
- 1 dozen prefolded cloth diapers
- 6 assorted stuffed animals
- Assorted baby clothing (we used 6 pairs of socks, 2 bibs, 1 cap, 2 rompers, and 1 plastic diaper cover)
- 3 yards of ¼"-wide pale yellow satin ribbon
- Travel-size baby toiletries
- T-pins
- Tape
- White thread
- 5"-long needle
- 10" round corrugated cake base

INSTRUCTIONS
For the center of the cake, glue the three plastic-foam circles together.

Press the diapers to remove any folds and wrinkles. To make a diaper roll, fold up 4" on one long edge to the front of the diaper, creating a pocket (Step 1 *below*). Fold the remaining long edge to the back of the diaper so it is even with the first fold (Step 2 *below*). The folded

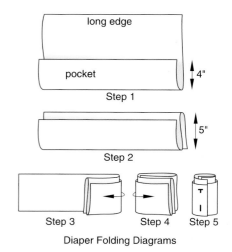

Diaper Folding Diagrams

diaper should be about 5" tall. With the pocket side down, fold the diaper in thirds, bringing in the short edges of the diaper (Steps 3 and 4). Bring the last two folds together at the center back; secure the roll with T-pins (Step 5). Repeat to make a total of 11 diaper rolls.

Use baby clothing and toiletries to decorate the diaper rolls as desired. Neatly fold the romper to the same height as the roll. Wrap the folded romper around the roll; secure with a T-pin at the back. Tie a length of satin ribbon into a bow around the middle of the romper. Wrap a folded diaper cover around a roll; tape in place. Wrap a bib around the front of a roll; pin in place. Stuff a toiletry or pair of socks into a pocket, slip a cap on a roll, or tie a satin ribbon bow around the center of a roll.

For the bottom layer, arrange seven decorated rolls around the sides of the plastic-foam center. Use T-pins to anchor the rolls to the

center. Thread the 5" needle with a long piece of white thread; knot together the thread ends. Sew the diapers together near the top edges. Pull the thread taut and knot. Repeat near the bottom edges.

For the top layer, arrange four decorated rolls on the top surface of the plastic-foam center. Use T-pins to anchor the rolls to the top surface of the center. Sew the diapers together as for the first layer.

For the cake top, fold the remaining diaper as shown in Steps 1 and 2. Gather the short edges of the diaper together in your hand and stuff into the center of the top layer, shaping the diaper to look like a collar. Sew the diaper in place. Place a stuffed animal inside the collar shape; sew in place.

Arrange the remaining stuffed animals around the bottom layer of the cake; sew them to the rolls. Stuff any extra socks around the cake. To provide stability, slip the corrugated cake base underneath the diaper cake.♥

Designer: Mary Jo Hiney
Photographer: Craig Anderson

personalized baby accessories

Shown *right* and on *pages 42–43*.

MATERIALS

- 10×7×6" plastic basket
- 4-oz. baby bottle
- 3"-diameter plain Christmas ornament
- Permanent paint pens in white and assorted pastel colors
- Tracing paper
- Transfer paper

INSTRUCTIONS

Trace the desired patterns, *below*. Use transfer paper to transfer the outlines of the pattern to the appropriate item. Trace the outlines with paint pens. If desired, add the child's name, birth date, or other personal information. Allow to dry. ♥

Designer: Cut-It-Up
Photographer: Craig Anderson

Christmas ornament patterns

Baby bottle patterns

Plastic bucket patterns

INSTRUCTIONS

Trace the pattern, *below.* Tape it on a light box or a brightly lit window. Place the front of the bodice over the tracing and use the erasable marker to trace it onto the garment. Working between the bodice and the lining, stitch the floss satin and stem stitches first. Then stitch the Japanese leaf stitches; embellish with blue-green floss veins. Embroider the French knot buds and the spider web roses next. If desired, attach the cross charm as indicated by the X on the chart. Cut a 5" length of blue silk ribbon and thread it through the fabric just above the cross and tie in a small bow; trim the ends. ❤

Designer: Alice Okon
Photographer: Marcia Cameron

ribbon embroidered christening overlay

Shown *above* and on *page 44.*

MATERIALS

- Purchased white linen bodice
- Cotton embroidery floss
- Tracing paper
- Silk ribbon
- Erasable marker
- Needle
- Embroidery hoop
- Cross charm
- White sewing thread

Anchor	DMC	
STEM STITCH		
1042	504	Blue-green (2X)
STRAIGHT STITCH		
1042	504	Blue-green (2X)
SATIN STITCH		
159	3841	Baby blue (2X)
JAPANESE LEAF STITCH		
	131	YLI Green 4mm silk ribbon
	157	YLI Pink 4mm silk ribbon
SPIDER WEB ROSE		
	156	YLI Light yellow 4mm silk ribbon
	157	YLI Pink 4mm silk ribbon
FRENCH KNOT		
	125	YLI Blue 4mm silk ribbon
	156	YLI Light yellow 4mm silk ribbon
	157	YLI Pink 4mm silk ribbon
ATTACHMENT		
X		Cross charm

transfer-embellished children's clothing

The finished blocks measure 3½×2¼" to 5½×6½". Shown *opposite* and on *page 45*.

MATERIALS

The items shown are handsewn, but the decorative blocks could also be added to purchased clothing.

For jumper or overall
- Commercial jumper or overall pattern
- Yardage and notions as noted on pattern
- 6—1"-diameter buttons

For hat
- Commercial brimmed hat pattern
- Yardage and notions as noted on pattern
- ¼ yard of fabric for bias trim

For child's artwork block
- Child's artwork
- 8"×10" rectangle each of muslin and freezer paper
- .05 permanent black marking pen
- Crayons
- White typing paper

For photo transfer block
- Purchased photo transfer or old postcard, photo-transfer paper, and muslin

INSTRUCTIONS

sewing

Sew the jumper or overall following the pattern manufacturer's instructions. If the pattern you use does not have buttonholes at the bottom of the bodice, simply sew the buttons evenly spaced along the front and back bottom edges. Measure the bodice to determine the size of block it can accommodate, and plan the artwork or photo accordingly. Complete the block as instructed below and blind-stitch in place on the bodice front.

Sew the hat following the pattern manufacturer's instructions. Measure the brim to determine the size of block it can accommodate, and plan the artwork or photo accordingly. Complete the block as instructed below and blind-stitch in place on the brim front. For the binding, cut a 2"-wide bias strip long enough to go around the brim. Fold the strip in

half lengthwise with wrong sides together; press. Pin the binding to the brim, aligning the raw edges of the binding with the finished edge of the brim. Fold over the beginning of the binding ½", and sew through all layers ¼" from the raw edges. Fold the binding over the brim edge; slip-stitch the pressed edge in place.

transfer the design

The decorative blocks on the clothing items were transferred in different ways. The artwork was transferred onto muslin with a permanent marking pen and crayons. The postcard transfers were purchased, but you can transfer images using photo-transfer paper. Both methods are described below.

child's artwork

Place the freezer paper, wax side up, on an ironing board. Lay pressed muslin on freezer paper and iron the freezer paper to the muslin.

Ask a child to color a picture on the stabilized muslin. Or, using a light box or a bright window, put the child's artwork behind the paper-backed muslin and trace the design onto the muslin with the permanent black marking pen. Color the design with crayons.

To heat-set the drawing, place the paper-backed muslin, crayon side up, on ironing board and cover with a sheet of white typing paper. Using a hot iron, with no steam, iron over design. To avoid color blurring, do not move the typing paper while ironing. Trim the design to desired shape and size, adding ¼" seam allowances. Remove freezer paper from muslin.

photo-transfer

Following the directions on the photo-transfer paper package, use a color photocopy machine to print a postcard or a child's drawing onto a sheet of photo-transfer paper. (Or take the postcard or drawing to a copy center and ask them to copy the image onto your photo-transfer paper.) Set the copier to mirror image unless you want the final drawing to be reversed.

Cut a piece of muslin for the photo-transfer paper. Following the photo-transfer paper instructions, apply the image to the muslin. (Or take the photo-transfer paper copy and muslin to a T-shirt shop with a heat press.) Trim the image to desired shape and size, adding ¼" seam allowances.

sew the fabric block

From coordinating fabric, cut 1¼"-wide strips for the bodice block and 1"-wide strips for the hat block. With right sides together, sew strips to the left and right edges of image, using a ¼" seam allowance. Press the seam allowances away from the image. Sew strips to the top and bottom edges and press in the same manner.

Using the pieced front as a pattern, cut one backing from the coordinating fabric. Sew the front and backing together with right sides facing, using a ¼" seam allowance. Trim the seams, and clip the corners. Cut a small slit in the backing about 1" above the bottom edge. Turn right side out through the slit; press. ❤

Designer: Jan Ballagh
Photographer: Marcia Cameron

redwork hanging supply bag

Finished size is 29×19". Shown *above* and on *pages 46–47*.

MATERIALS
- 1 yard of 54"-wide red-and-ecru home decorator fabric
- ⅝ yard of 54"-wide ecru duck
- ¼ yard of 54"-wide chenille
- ⅝ yard of 45"-wide needlepunch cotton batting
- Red embroidery floss
- ⅛ yard of ⅛"-diameter red cording
- 1¼"-diameter red button
- Tracing paper
- Transfer marker
- Tailor's chalk or other erasable marker

INSTRUCTIONS

cut the fabrics

From red-and-ecru fabric, cut one 28½×18½" back, two 9½×22½" large pockets, a 4×24" handle, a 3¼×19" bottom binding strip, and enough 3¼"-wide strips to total 75".

From solid ecru duck, cut one 28½×18½" front, two 1¾×19" binding strips for the small pockets, and a 1½×19" strip for the bottom edge of the upper pocket.

From chenille fabric, cut two 6½×22½" small pockets and two 1¾×19" binding strips for the large pockets.

Referring to Diagram 1, layer the duck front and the red-and-ecru fabric back. Fold the layered fabrics in half lengthwise. On the edge opposite the fold, measure and mark the point that is 7" from the top. Draw a line that connects the mark with the fold at the top; cut along the line and round the resulting corners.

embroidery

Separate the duck front from the red-and-ecru back. Trace the embroidery pattern onto tracing paper with the transfer marker. On the ironing board, center the tracing, ink side down, at the top of the duck front with the tip of the center bird's tail 2½" below the center point of the front. Following manufacturer's directions, transfer the design. Use two strands of red floss to outline stitch the design. Press.

pockets

With right sides facing, stitch a 1¾×19" chenille pocket-binding strip to upper edge of large pocket, using a ¼" seam allowance. Press seam towards binding. Fold binding to inside and turn raw edge under ¼". Pin in place. Stitch. Press binding. Repeat with the remaining large pocket. Stitch the 1¾×19" solid ecru pocket binding strips to the upper edges of the small pockets in the same manner.

With right sides up, layer the small pockets atop the large pockets, aligning one long edge and the side edges to make a pocket unit. Referring to Diagram 2, mark the stitching lines (indicated on the diagram by dashed lines) and pleat lines (indicated on the diagram by dashed and dotted lines).

On the duck front, mark a placement line for the bottom edge of the upper pocket. Mark stitching lines 5¼" from each edge.

Pin one pocket unit to the duck front, aligning the bottom edges and the stitching lines. The center section of the pocket unit will have about 2" of slack. Align the bottom edge of

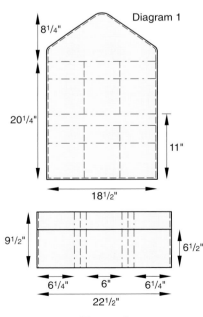

Diagram 1

Diagram 2

the other pocket unit with the placement line on the duck front. Also align the stitching lines. Sew along each of the four stitching lines, backstitching at the top and bottom of each pocket unit.

Fold the pleat lines to the stitching lines and pin at the bottom of each pleat. Align the sides of the pocket units with the sides of the duck front and pin.

Machine-baste each pocket unit to the duck front along the sides and bottom using a ¼" seam allowance.

Anchor   DMC
STEM STITCH
    9046 / 321 Christmas Red
SATIN STITCH
    9046 ⧚ 321 Christmas Red
FRENCH KNOT
    9046 • 321 Christmas Red

With right sides facing, sew the 1½×19" strip to bind the bottom edge of the upper pockets to the bottom edge of the upper pockets, using a ¼" seam allowance. Press seam towards binding. Turn raw edge under ¼" and stitch in place.

handle

Press the handle edges under ½" on both long edges. Press handle in half, matching long edges. Topstitch through both layers close to fold on each long edge. Pin handle on right side of red-and-ecru back just below the diagonal curve. Pin the ends of the cord to the top of the back about ¾" from the center.

finishing

Layer the duck front, right side up, on the batting. Trim the batting to the shape of the front. Place back on work surface, wrong side up. Layer batting and front on the back. Pin layers together, taking extra care at

all edges. Sew through all layers along the upper pocket stitching lines again, stopping short of the pleats at the bottom of the pockets. Pin layers together, taking extra care at all edges.

With wrong sides together, fold the bottom binding strip in half lengthwise and press. Align the raw edges and sew the binding strip to the right side of the bottom edge of the layered bag, using a ⅜" seam allowance. Press binding towards bottom edge. Fold binding around to the back and hand-stitch the folded edge of the binding to the back.

Sew the short edges of the remaining binding strips together to make one long piece and use it to bind the remaining edges in the same manner as the bottom, folding the ends under ½" and making sure to catch the ends of the handle and cording into the stitching.

Fold up the finished bag and sew the button under the cording loop.♥

Designer: Mary Jo Hiney
Photographer: Scott Little

GIFTS
kids
CAN make

Kids, with plenty of talent and time on their *hands,* can make personal gifts Mom, Dad, and the whole family will *remember.* Younger ones might require the supervision of a parent or older sibling. That makes the gift-giving— and *crafting*—more of a family affair!

Easy Throw and Pillowcase start on *page 70.*

Here's a *delightful* duo for gift-giving, *right.* Encourage a young child to share a favorite *drawing.* Then use photo-transfer techniques to incorporate them into a *personal* gift. The straight-line seams of this pillow cover and throw make it a natural project for older kids.

Dad's *travel kit, below*, is a purchased box covered
with cut-paper puzzle pieces. These are done with a template,
but *kids* can design their own or trace pieces
from a real jigsaw *puzzle*.

DAD'S TRAVEL KIT

**Dad's Travel Kit
starts on *page 72*.**

Right: **Painted Garden Stakes
start on *page 72*.**

Kids want a *"stake"* in the gifts they give, so let them take part in preparing
these outstanding *garden* posts, *right*. They can paint the purchased
wooden stakes and plaques and help attach the *door knobs* from which the
finished vegetable and flower plaques will hang.

Sewing Box
starts on *page 73.*

Moms who *patch* blue jeans, mend socks,
and fix small tears need a *box* to hold the tools
of their trade. This petite sewing kit,
above, does it with fabric, glue, a bit of fiberfill,
and a button. Sized to carry thread, embroidery
scissors, and other small *sewing notions,*
the box has a padded lid for holding
pins and needles.

Present the sewing box to Mom with lunch,
served on a brightly colored mat, *right,*
assembled from *fabric strips,* folded
together to become a colorful tabletop
accessory. There's no sewing involved!
It's all done with an iron (under adult
supervision) and easy *weaving*
and folding techniques.

**Woven Place Mat
starts on *page 74*.**

Simply Seashells
start on *page 74.*

Ready, set, *stamp* away! Really cool stationery
like this, *below*, is perfect for parents and older
siblings. It takes only *minutes,* too, with pigment ink
pads and assorted rubber stamps. Thread a
neat touch of *ribbon* through circles punched on
each side of the shell design.

Seaside Stationary
starts on *page 75.*

Set a *seashell*
collection to all sorts
of things, and see
what new *treasures*
you'll discover!
With glue, kids can attach shells, as thick as
barnacles on a ship, to picture frames,
candles—whatever their hearts *desire,*
above and *at left.*

easy throw and pillowcase

Finished throw is 39×58½".
Finished pillowcase is 22½×32".
Shown *above* and on *page 62–63*.

MATERIALS

- Child's drawing(s)
- 8 sheets of photo-transfer paper
- 1 yard of 200 thread count muslin
- 1¼ yards *each* of five homespun plaids
- ¼ yard of gold fabric
- 1⅔ yards of backing fabric for throw
- ⅔ yard of homespun plaid for binding for throw
- 45×64" of quilt batting for throw
- 8—1" buttons for covering

INSTRUCTIONS

Quantities specified are for 44/45" wide, 100% cotton fabrics. All measurements include a ¼" seam allowance.

make photo transfers

Following directions on the photo-transfer paper package, use a color photocopier to print a child's drawing onto each sheet of photo-transfer paper. (Or take the drawing(s) to a photo copy shop and ask them to transfer the drawings.) Set the copier to mirror image unless you want the final drawing(s) to be reversed.

Cut a piece of muslin for each photo-transfer copy; leave about 1" excess around all edges. Following the photo-transfer paper instructions, apply the photos to the muslin.

cut the fabrics

To make the best use of your fabrics, cut the pieces in the order that follows. Cut all strips across the width of the fabric. Make templates of Pattern A and Pattern B.

From homespun plaids, cut:
- 5—8×39" rectangles for throw
- 5 of Pattern A for throw
- 3—8×14" rectangles for pillowcase

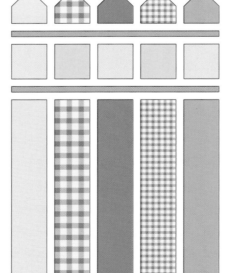

Throw Diagram

- 1—23×25" rectangle for pillowcase back
- 2—16½×23" hem rectangles for pillowcase

From gold fabric, cut:
- 2—2¼×38" strips for throw
- 2—2¼×23" strips for pillowcase

From homespun plaid binding fabric, cut:
- 6—3½×42" strips
- 8 of Pattern B

Trim each photo transfer to 8×8".

assemble the throw

Referring to the Throw Diagram for placement, lay out the five 8×39" rectangles, two 2¼×38" gold strips, five photo transfers, and the five A homespun pieces. Sew together the photo transfers and homespun plaid pieces into rows. Press seam allowances open. Alternating with the gold strips, sew the rows together. Press seam allowances in one direction.

complete the throw

Layer the quilt top, batting, and backing. With contrasting thread, quilt ¼" on each side of each seam.

Sew the homespun print 3½×42" strips together with diagonal seams to form one long binding strip. Trim the excess fabric, leaving ¼" seam allowances. Press the seam allowances open. With wrong sides together, fold the binding strip in half lengthwise and press. Beginning in the center of one long side of the quilt, place the binding strip against the back side of the quilt top, aligning the binding strip's raw edge with the quilt top's raw edge. Fold over the beginning of the binding strip about ½". Sew around the quilt, mitering the corners. Press the binding to the right side and topstitch along the seam line.

For one tab, sew two B pieces together, leaving a small opening in

one long edge. Trim points. Turn the tabs right side out. Topstitch close to edge. Repeat to make four tabs.

With homespun scraps, cover eight 1" buttons, following package instructions.

Referring to the photograph, sew the covered buttons over tabs at the inner corner of each top point.

assemble the pillowcase

Sew together the long edges of three 8×14" homespun rectangles. Then sew together the three remaining photo transfers in a row. Press the seams in one direction. Referring to the Pillowcase Front Diagram for placement, lay out the homespun rectangle row, the two 2¼×23" gold strips, the photo transfer row, and one 16½×23" homespun pillowcase hem rectangle. Sew the photo transfers and homespun plaid pieces together into rows. Press seam allowances open. Alternating with the gold strips, sew the rows together. Press seam allowances toward the hem rectangle. With contrasting thread, machine-stitch ¼" beyond both sides of each seam.

For the back, sew the 23" edges of the remaining pieces together. Press the seam allowances toward the hem rectangle. With right sides together, sew the pillowcase front and back together on the sides and bottom. Turn right side out.

On the open hem end, press ¼" to wrong side, then press 8" to wrong side, forming hem. Machine stitch close to fold. ❤

Designer: Jim Williams
Photographer: Marcia Cameron and Scott Little

Pattern A
Cut 5

Fold

Pattern B
Cut 4

Fold

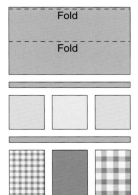

Pillowcase Front Diagram

Pillowcase Back Diagram

dad's travel kit

Box measures 12½×10½×5½".
Shown *above* and on *page 64.*

MATERIALS
- Large memory box
- 1" sponge brush
- Delta Ceramcoat Acry-Blend
- Plastic wrap
- Coluzzle oval template kit
- Old map or wrapping paper that looks like a map
- Pictures of vehicles from a magazine
- Decoupage medium
- White dimensional fabric paint
- Travel items: maps, brochures, bottled water, and travel guides

Delta Ceramcoat Colors
- AB Autumn Brown 2055
- BU Burnt Umber 2025

INSTRUCTIONS
Use the sponge brush to base-coat all of the outer surfaces of the unassembled box with two coats of AB; let paint dry.

Apply one coat of Acry-blend drying retarder to the painted surfaces of the box. Quickly apply one coat of BU to the prepared surfaces. To add grain lines, press a scrunched piece of plastic wrap down on the wet paint, then lift up the wrap. Continue to cover the entire painted surface of the box with grain lines. When the paint is completely dry, assemble the box.

Using the puzzle template, cut out one oval puzzle and approximately 30 additional puzzle pieces from the map or wrapping paper.

Position the oval puzzle on the front of the box; cut the pieces along the bottom of the lid. Remove the oval puzzle pieces from the box and apply decoupage medium to that area. Use your fingers to press the puzzle pieces in place on the wet area, smoothing from the center out to remove bubbles and adhere edges. Add additional puzzle pieces and vehicle photos, one at a time, randomly over the box; let dry.

Apply two coats of decoupage medium to the entire box, letting dry between coats.

Use the white dimensional marker to write "Dad's Travel Kit" on the front of the lid; let dry. Fill the box with travel items. ♥

Designer: Sandy Payne
Photographer: Craig Anderson and Marcia Cameron

painted garden stakes

Signs measure 8×5" and stakes are 36" tall. Shown *below* and on *page 65.*

MATERIALS
- 8×5" pieces of ¼" plywood for signs
- 36" tall garden stakes from a nursery or lumber yard
- Sandpaper and tack cloth
- White chalk
- Toothpicks
- Old door knobs
- Screws
- Drill and pliers
- 18" lengths of 11-gauge wire
- Brushes: 2" foam, #2 round

Delta Ceramcoat Colors
- Black 2506
- CL Coral 2044
- NA Napa Wine 2443
- OY Olive Yellow 2493
- PN Pine Green 2526
- SE Seminole Green 2009
- SW Straw 2078
- TA Tangerine 2043
- TS Tomato Spice 2098
- White 2505

INSTRUCTIONS
Lightly sand the stakes and the signs, concentrating on the edges. Remove the sanding dust with a tack cloth.

Apply one coat of paint to the stakes and the front surface of the signs, using PN for the stakes and any of the suggested colors listed above for the signs. To achieve a rustic look, do not cover the wood completely. Let the paint dry.

Use white chalk to freehand draw the lettering on the sign. Paint over the chalk lines with the tip of a round brush and desired paint. To make dots, dip fingertip in paint and touch on the sign. To make seeds, paint black teardrop shapes. When black is dry, use a toothpick to add a white highlight dot to each seed.

When the paint is dry, attach an old doorknob to each stake with a screw, approximately 1½" from the top of stake.

Drill holes through the sign ¼" below the top edge and ¾" from the side edges. To hang, insert wire ends through the holes; use pliers to twist ends around wire. Hang the sign from the knob on stake. 💙

Designer: Shara Reiner
Photographer: Craig Anderson

sewing box

Box measures 6" in diameter.
Shown *at right* and on *page 66.*

MATERIALS
- 6"-diameter round papier-mâché box
- 8" square of high-loft batting
- ¼ yard print fabric
- 8" square of coordinating solid fabric
- Tape measure
- Glue gun and hotmelt adhesive
- Crafts glue and dish
- 1" sponge brush
- Scraps of felt
- Pinking shears
- 1⅛"-diameter self-cover button form
- Strong thread and needle
- 1"-wide grosgrain ribbon
- Two large eyelets
- Awl
- 1 yard of 1"-wide satin ribbon

INSTRUCTIONS
Trace the box lid, top down, on the wrong side of the batting; cut out. Trace the box lid on the solid color fabric; cut out the lid shape, adding a ½" margin. Use a tape measure to determine the circumference of the lid; add 1" for overlap. Measure the height of the lid; multiply this number by 4. Use these measurements to cut a strip of print fabric for the sides of the lid.

Measure the circumference of the box base; add 1" for overlap. Measure the height of the base; add 1½". Use these measurements to cut a piece of print fabric for the base.

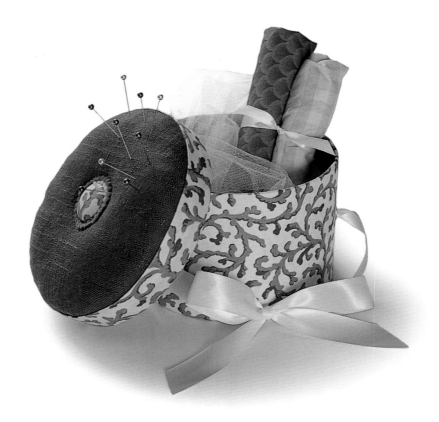

Glue the batting centered on the lid. Center the circle of solid fabric on the batting-covered lid. Glue the margins to the lid sides, smoothing the fabric over the batting.

For the lid sides, fold the print fabric strip in half and glue onto the lid sides with the folded edge even with the top edge of the lid. To overlap the ends, fold under ½" and glue in place. Clip the excess fabric at 1" intervals from the raw edge to the bottom of the lid. Fold the clipped fabric to the inside of the lid and glue in place.

Cover the button form with a scrap of print fabric, following the button manufacturer's instructions. Use a pinking shears to cut two felt circles slightly larger than the button. Center the felt circles and button on the box lid. Use strong thread to sew the button to the lid, knotting the thread securely on the underside of the lid.

Mix crafts glue and a few drops of water in a dish until the glue is the consistency of light cream. Use the sponge brush to apply an even coat of diluted glue to the sides of the box base. Press the print fabric rectangle onto the base sides, keeping an even margin of fabric at the top and bottom for tabs. To overlap, fold under ½" at one end of rectangle and glue over the opposite raw edge. Fold the margins into the box at the top and onto the bottom of the base, clipping a tab every 1"; glue the tabs down. Glue the grosgrain ribbon to inside of base, covering the tabs.

To attach the eyelets, use an awl to make holes in opposite sides of the base, approximately 2" from the bottom. Glue the deep half of the eyelets in the holes. Cut the satin ribbon into two 18" lengths. Tie a knot at one end of each satin ribbon length. Thread the opposite ends of the ribbons through the eyelets from the inside of the box. Place the lid on the base and tie the satin ribbon at the top of lid. 💙

Designer: Jim Williams
Photographers: Craig Anderson and Marcia Cameron

woven fabric mat

Mat measures 13" square.
Shown above and on *pages 66–67*.

MATERIALS
- 6—18" squares of fabric
- Iron and ironing board
- Buttons
- Embroidery floss and needle or glue

INSTRUCTIONS
Cut the fabrics into a total of 24—4×18" strips. To prepare the strips for weaving, press each strip in half lengthwise with wrong sides facing. Open up the strip. Fold each long edge to the center of the strip; press. Fold the strip in half again, concealing the long raw edges. The strip should be 1" wide.

Lay 12 strips vertically, side by side, on a flat surface, making sure that the single-fold edge faces out on the left and right strip. Weave the remaining strips over and under the vertical strips, leaving at least 2" long tails at each end and making sure that the single-fold edge faces out on the top and bottom strip. Trim all tails to 2".

Working around the mat, fold every-other tail up and over the closest outer strip, tucking the end of the tail between the folds of the outer strip. Press as you work. Turn the mat over and repeat for the remaining tails. Fold and tuck the corner tails in the same manner. Referring to the photo, *above,* sew or glue buttons to the front of the mat.♥

Designer: Laura Collins
Photographer: Craig Anderson

fringed foam mat

Mat measures11½×7½".
Shown on at *left*.

MATERIALS
- 2 or more sheets of 11×17½" colored foam
- Ruler
- Pencil and scissors or rotary cutter and self-healing mat
- 40 brass brads

INSTRUCTIONS
Use a ruler, pencil, and scissors to cut 13—1×11½" strips and 9—1×17½" strips from the colored foam. Or, have an adult cut the strips with a ruler, rotary cutter, and mat. Lay the long strips side by side on a flat surface. Weave the short strips over and under the long strips, alternating the colors as desired and leaving a 1" tail at each end. To hold the strips in place, press a brad through the woven strips all around the outer edges. Trim the tails even.♥

Designer: Laura Collins
Photographer: Marcia Cameron

simply seashells

linen-wrapped shell frame
Frame measures 8×6". Shown *opposite* and on *pages 68–69*.

MATERIALS
- Small oval frame
- Natural linen twine
- 4 round spiral shells
- Glue gun and hotmelt adhesive

INSTRUCTIONS
Cut about a 1-yard length of twine. Glue one end of the twine to the frame back; wrap the twine around the frame. Glue end of twine to the frame back. Continue wrapping 1 yard lengths around the frame in this manner to cover completely. Glue shells centered on the sides of the frame.

shell candles
Shown *opposite* and on *pages 68–69*.

MATERIALS
- Pillar candle
- Assorted shells
- Glue gun and hotmelt adhesive
- Stiff cardboard (optional)

INSTRUCTIONS

Glue shells to the candle around the base. Or, cut a cardboard base about 1½" greater in diameter than the candle. Glue the base to the bottom of the candle. Glue shells around the candle, securing them to both the base and the candle.

linen and shell frame

Frame measures 7×10". Shown on *pages 68–69*.

MATERIALS

- 7×10" unfinished flat wooden frame with a 4½×7½" opening
- 10×13" rectangle of natural linen
- Spray adhesive
- 7 scallop shells
- Glue gun and hot melt adhesive

INSTRUCTIONS

Lightly spray the wrong side of the linen with adhesive, being careful not to saturate the fabric. With the adhesive side down, center the linen over the front of the frame. Use your fingers to press the linen onto the frame, smoothing out any wrinkles. Fold the linen onto the sides and back of the frame, creasing at the edges and neatly folding at the corners.

Cut a large X at the center of the linen, cutting from the corners of the frame opening to make triangle-shaped flaps. Fold the flaps to the back of the frame, creasing along the edges.

Glue shells to the corners of the frame, covering any exposed wood at the corners of the frame opening. Glue the remaining shells centered on the sides of the frame.

linen-wrapped candle

Shown on *pages 68–69*.

MATERIALS

- Pillar candle
- Natural linen twine
- Natural-colored rubber band to fit candle
- Scallop shell
- Glue gun and hotmelt adhesive

INSTRUCTIONS

Place the rubber band around the candle about ¼" from the bottom. Tuck one end of the twine under the rubber band to secure. Tightly wrap twine around the candle, stopping about 1¼" from the top. Glue end of twine to the wrapped twine. Glue the shell to the center front of candle, covering the end of twine. ♥

Designer: Jim Williams
Photographer: Perry Struse

seaside stationary

Shown *below* and on *page 69*.

MATERIALS

- Assorted sheets of stationary and envelopes
- Fish and shell rubber stamps
- Coordinating stamp pads
- 6" lengths of ¼"-wide satin ribbon
- Hole punch
- Crafts glue

INSTRUCTIONS

For the fish stationary, use two coordinating stamp pads to randomly stamp fish on the bottom quarter of the sheet paper and the envelope flap. Stamp one fish on the back of the envelope below the flap.

For the shell stationary, stamp a single shell centered along the bottom of the sheet paper about ½" above the bottom edge. Stamp one shell centered on the envelope flap with the top of the shell extending beyond the top of the envelope. To add ribbon accents, punch holes through the sheet and envelope flap on each side of the stamped shell. Trim the ribbon ends at an angle. Insert the ribbon ends through the holes from the back to the front. Use a dot of glue to secure the ribbon on the back of sheet and flap. ♥

Designer: Jim Williams
Photographer: Perry Struse

Left: Memory Frame starts on *page 81.*

Below right: Grandmother's Handwork starts on *page 81.* Button Frame starts on *page 82.*

FOR moms AND dads

Gifts that are *handmade* lend a warm feeling to any celebration. Whether it's a *parent's* (or grandparent's) birthday or their special day in May, June, or September, *honor* your mother, father, or grandparent with one of these great ideas.

Like the pages in a *memory* scrapbook, these frames display *treasures* that have particular meaning for you and your mother. Lovely to look at, these memento frames might include a piece of her handwork, a *sentimental* card sent long ago, or buttons from a coat she made especially for you.

**Golf Wreath
starts on *page 82.***

Tee-off your birthday gift-giving with one any
pro will love. Perfect for Dad's or Mom's office or den,
this golfer's *wreath,* sports silk ivy, spagnum and
Spanish mosses, golf balls, crossed clubs,
and *divots* of reindeer moss.

Reel in the compliments and your parent's appreciation when you present this
painted beauty, *right.* Starting as a plain, two-drawer box, it becomes the *catch*
of the day with a big ol' *fish* and fishing lures for decoration.

Fishing Lure Box starts on *page 83.*

To *brighten* quiet spaces,
hammered *copper* wire takes a
decorative turn. It curls around
three *votive* cups for candle or
flower holders that stand alone
or hang from a wall.

**Copper Votive Holders
start on *page 81.***

copper votive holders

Holders measure 5" to 11" tall.
Shown on *page 80*.

MATERIALS

For each holder:

- 1' length of copper grounding wire (or 6- to 8-gauge copper wire)
- Needle-nose pliers
- Heavy-duty tin snips or wire cutters
- Glass votive cup
- Hammer
- Drill and metal bit
- 18-gauge copper wire
- Round and teardrop crystals

INSTRUCTIONS

Beginning with the top of the holder, use the pliers to hold the grounding wire as you bend the wire into a pleasing curved shape.

After you've finished shaping the top of the holder, hold the votive cup at the end of the curved shape on a flat surface. Wrap the wire around the base of the cup about one and a half times to support it. Continue to wrap the wire around the bottom of the cup, curling the wire into the center. Cut off any excess wire.

Remove the cup and use the hammer to flatten 1" at the top end of the holder. Drill a hole through the flattened area to accommodate the 18-gauge wire. Attach a crystal through the drilled hole at the top of holder with 18-gauge wire. ♥

Designer: Susan Hinds Bassman
Photographer: Craig Anderson

memory frame

Frame measures 15×18". Shown *above* and on *pages 76–77*.

MATERIALS

- Old large oval frame
- White acrylic paint
- Paintbrush
- Fine-grit sandpaper
- Tack cloth
- Pearl buttons
- Crafts glue
- Foam-core board cut to fit frame opening
- Memorabilia, such as embroidered tea towel, flat lace, and antique card
- Acid-free adhesive

INSTRUCTIONS

Apply a coat of white paint to frame. When the paint is dry, rub frame with sandpaper to remove as much paint as desired. Wipe off the sanding dust with a tack cloth. Glue the buttons to the frame.

Referring to the photographs for ideas, plan the placement of the memorabilia pieces. Mount them on the foam-core board with adhesive and insert in the frame. ♥

Designer: Judy Nielson
Photographer: Craig Anderson

grandmother's handwork

Frame measures 7" square.
Shown *below* and on *page 77*.

MATERIALS

- Old frame
- 2 complementary mat boards cut to fit frame opening
- Small round doily
- Acid-free adhesive
- Old photo or color copy of photo
- Scrap of coordinating acid-free paper

INSTRUCTIONS

Cut a ¾"-wide mat from the mat board selected for the top. From the center portion of this mat board, trim off a scant ¼" from each edge.

Center the doily on the trimmed square of mat board, using a small amount of adhesive. Cut the photo into a circle. From the scrap paper, cut a circle about ½" larger than the photo. Use adhesive to attach the layers and to center on the doily.

Position the ¾"-wide mat and the assembled center square on the second mat board; secure with adhesive. Insert mats in the frame. ♥

Designer: Judy Nielson
Photographer: Craig Anderson

embellished button mirror

Mirror measures 5×7".
Shown *above* and on *page 77*.

MATERIALS
- 5×7" oval mirror
- Sheet of white paper
- Assorted large buttons (we used 24—1⅛- to 1⅝"-diameter pansy akoya shell)
- 1 easel back to fit mirror
- E-6000 Glue

INSTRUCTIONS
Trace the mirror shape onto a sheet of white paper. Position the buttons on the traced shape, overlapping the buttons slightly, until you are pleased with the arrangement. This will allow you to move, add, subtract, or change the arrangement easily and to glue the buttons one at a time to the right place on the mirror.

Use small amounts of E-6000 to glue the buttons onto the front of the mirror, starting with the buttons that are underneath adjacent buttons. Keep the mirror flat while gluing so buttons will not slide. Let the glue dry for 24 hours and until the buttons feel firmly attached.

Position the easel on the mirror back so the mirror stands securely at the right angle. Mark the position of the easel on the mirror back; glue in place. Lay the mirror flat with the button side down; let dry for 24 hours. ♥

Designer: Carole Cree
Photographer: Craig Anderson

golf wreath

Wreath measures 18" in diameter.
Shown *below* and *page 78*.

MATERIALS
- 18"-diameter grapevine wreath
- 7 golf balls and tees
- 2 golf clubs
- Sheet moss
- Reindeer moss
- Spanish moss
- Silk ivy bush
- Red starflowers
- Glue gun and hotmelt adhesive
- 18-gauge floral wire
- Wire cutters
- Floral tape

INSTRUCTIONS
Hot glue the golf tees to the golf balls; set aside and allow glue to set.

Securely wire the golf clubs to the bottom right side of the wreath, referring to the photograph, *below*, for placement. For added stability, use green floral tape at the junction of the clubs.

Hot glue sheet moss in several places around the lower side of the wreath; let the glue set. Add reindeer and Spanish mosses in the same manner.

Cut leaves from the silk ivy bush. Randomly tuck ivy leaves into the moss, dabbing glue on the stems to secure in place. Cut the red star flowers into different lengths; sort the flowers into groups of three. Dab glue on the stem ends and stick the flower groups into the wreath. Hot glue the golf balls into the moss in a pleasing arrangement.

When you are satisfied with the placement of leaves, flowers, and golf balls, fill in any gaps with additional pieces of the mosses.

Use the wire to make a hanger on the center back of the wreath. ♥

Designer: Lenny Houts
Photographer: Craig Anderson

fishing lure box

Shown on *page 79*.

MATERIALS

- Purchased 8½×5½×8¾ wooden recipe box
- Wood sealer
- Fruitwood wood stain
- Satin-finish varnish
- Brushes: ¾" synthetic flat, #12 synthetic flat, #8 synthetic flat, #1 synthetic liner, spatter or old toothbrush

Delta Ceramcoat Colors
- Black 2506
- AN Antique Gold 2002
- AU Dark Burnt Umber 2527
- BD Bright Red 2503
- BG Black Green 2116
- CB Candy Bar 2407
- CH Charcoal 2436
- EY English Yew 2095
- OG Soft Grey 2515
- OP Old Parchment 2092
- QG Quaker Gray 2057
- SP Silver Pine 2534
- ST Spice Tan 2063
- TS Tomato Spice 2098
- White 2505

INSTRUCTIONS

prepare the box

Sand all surfaces with 100- and then 150-grit sandpaper. Remove the sanding dust with a tack cloth. Apply wood sealer to all surfaces, and let the sealer dry. Sand again with 150-grit sandpaper and wipe clean.

paint the pieces

Base-coat, shade, and highlight the design areas with #12 and #8 flat brushes, using the size that best fits the area. Paint details with a #1 liner brush.

Stain all surfaces of the box and the drawers with fruitwood wood stain. Let the stain dry. Dilute AU with water to ink consistency. Dip a spatter brush or an old toothbrush into the paint, and spatter the

outside surfaces of the box and the drawers. Let the paint dry.

Transfer the oval pattern to the top of the box. Using a ¾" flat brush and BG, paint the top of the box around the oval, and the box's front and bottom edges. Transfer the fish and lure patterns, *pages 84–85*.

fish

Base-coat the body and the tail fin EY. Paint over the fins on the body, but do not paint the other fins or inside the mouth. Base-coat the inside of the mouth QG. Dilute BG with water to ink consistency and, using a #1 liner brush, paint the spotted design along the back and

on the side of the fish. Float BG shading across the top and QG highlights along the bottom of the fish and on the end of the tail fin. Float CH shading inside the mouth along the right side.

Base-coat the fins SP and paint the eye AN. Dilute EY with water to ink consistency, and paint the detail lines on the fins. Using black thinned to ink consistency, outline the eye and paint the pupil. Dilute SP to ink consistency, and paint a wide line around the mouth. In the same manner, paint a BG line next to the SP line, and paint the detail

Continued

fishing lure box

lines on the tail fin. Float BG shading on and around all the SP fins, except the one on top.

red-and-white lure

Base-coat the front section BD and the back section OG. Referring to the photograph, *page 83,* use a liner brush to paint a QG line along the entire length of the bottom of the lure, extending slightly beyond the back and more beyond the front. Dilute Black with water to ink consistency, and paint a narrower line under the QG line.

Using the thinned Black and the tip of the liner brush, apply the dots on the top of the lure. Let the dots dry. Float CH shading along the top of the lure. Float back-to-back white highlights in the center of the lure. by first floating white in the center of the lure. Quickly flip the brush over and float again, placing the white

side of the brush next to the edge of the floated white. The strongest color will be in the center, and it will fade away on both sides.

red-and-yellow lure

Base-coat the front section TS and the back section OP. Float ST shading on the top and bottom edges of the yellow section. Float CB shading on the bottom and bottom edges of the red section. Float back-to-back white highlights in the center of the lure. Dilute OP with water to ink consistency and, using a liner brush, paint a circle for the eye. In the same manner, paint a Black circle around the OP circle.

hooks, propellers, and screw eyes

Base-coat QG. On the front propellers by the red and yellow lure, float CH shading on the back left side of the top propeller, and at the base of the

other propeller. Dilute CH with water to ink consistency, and paint a line in the curves of the hooks and the screw eyes, and on the underneath side of the shank of the hooks.

Using paint thinned to ink consistency, highlight with OG just above the shading in the curves of the hooks and the screw eyes and along the shank. Still using OG, paint a line on the upper right side of the top propeller, and float a highlight on the lower right side of the bottom propeller.

Dilute Black to ink consistency, and paint a thin line along the back edges of the back propellers.

finish the box

Apply two or more coats of varnish, allowing ample drying time between each coat.

Designer: Margaret Wilson
Photographer: Perry Struse

TOP DRAWER

BOTTOM DRAWER

TOP OF BOX

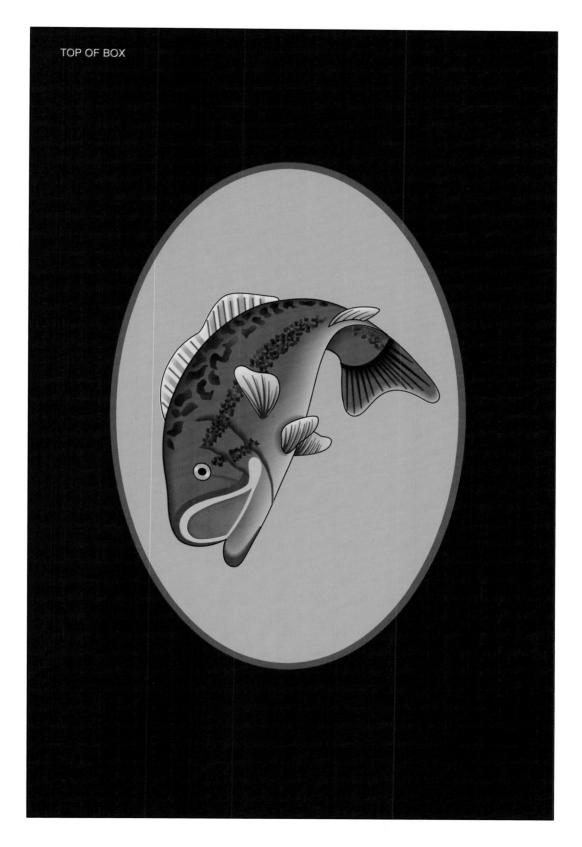

Below and right:
Stars-and-Stripes Garments
and Earrings start on *page 97.*

A year is filled with special *reasons*
for crafting presents—they're called
holidays. Inside this crafters' package,
you'll find all sorts of tokens and *treasures*
to *unwrap* at Easter, Independence Day, Halloween,
Thanksgiving, and Christmas.

CELEBRATE THE

holidays

Celebrate spring and summer holidays with *fast-finish* gifts
that say, "enjoy the season!" Fill a friend's summer holidays
with *patriotic* spirit without missing much outdoor fun!
Adorn a sweatshirt or shortall with some fusible red,
white, and blue *pizzazz.*

Patriotic Pots
start on *page 99.*

Waffle Bowl May Baskets
start on *page 96.*

When you're invited to celebrate a holiday,
say thank you with a *handmade* gift.
For summer parties, present your host with a
delightful terra-cotta trio, *left,* that dishes up
snacks and serves as a *patriotic* centerpiece, too.
Even kids can show their appreciation by creating
some *waffle* bowl May baskets, *top,* to share
with friends. Or use a few simple paints to turn
papier-mâché boxes into charming
Easter egg collectors, *below.*

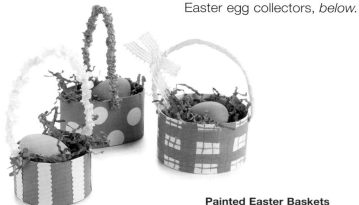

Painted Easter Baskets
start on *page 96.*

Left to right:
Jack-o'-Lantern-in-the-House
starts on *page 102.*

Fall Goodie Box
starts on *page 105.*

This year, give treats—and tricks—to all the little *hobgoblins*
that show up at your door. Deliver the treats in this delightful,
painted wooden box, *opposite right*, then hand them the trick
when this jack-o'-lantern pops from his haunted house,
opposite left. *"Jack"* is cleverly constructed from
a fabric-covered plastic-foam ball and dryer venting hose. He tucks comfortably
beneath the roof of the corrugated *mansion* until trick-or-treaters pull the string!

Place Card Treats
start on *page 106.*

Dispense tricks and treats with crafty *style.* If you're hosting a Halloween party,
fill a three-sided box with goodies and personalize it for a place card.
Easy-to-make candy-filled *cornucopias* will win *cheers*
from goblins of all ages.

Floral Horn of Plenty
starts on *page 107.*

Easy Patchwork Table Runner
starts on *page 108.*

Maple Leaf Favor
starts on *page 106*.

For a Thanksgiving host or hostess,
fill the *harvest* table to overflowing with
accessories every bit as *delicious*
as the *holiday* foods you'll enjoy.

Start with the handsome *patchwork* runner
and flower-filled cornucopia centerpiece,
left. Or bring a paper gift bag,
personalized with rubber stamps.

Snowy Winter Night
starts on *page 109.*

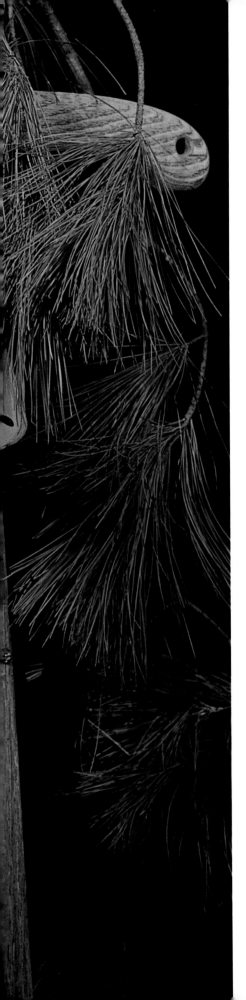

Show appreciation for a teacher, neighbor, or
dear friend with this *hand-painted* wall hanging, *left*.
The scene—warm friends set against a *snowy* moonlit night—
makes a welcoming door decoration. For fun,
paint the hollow of *spoons* and hang them from the
brass upholstery tacks set around the edge.

**Heart Mittens
start on *page 114*.**

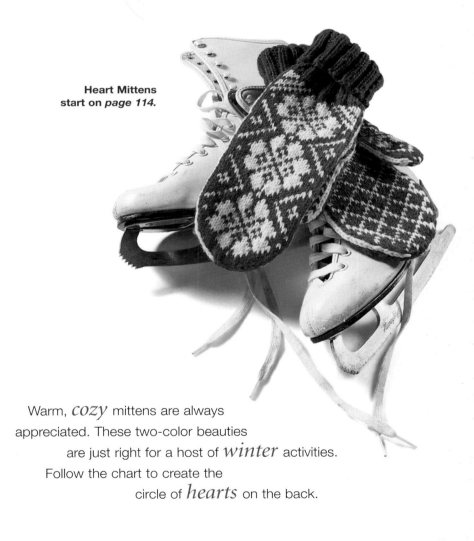

Warm, *cozy* mittens are always
appreciated. These two-color beauties
are just right for a host of *winter* activities.
Follow the chart to create the
circle of *hearts* on the back.

painted easter baskets

Baskets measure 3" and 4¼" round and 4¼" oval. Shown *above* and on *page 89*.

MATERIALS

For each basket
- Small papier-mâché box
- T-pin and nail
- Flat paintbrush
- 1 white chenille stem
- 18" length of ruched or wire-edged ribbon
- Glue gun and hotmelt adhesive

For plaid basket
- DecoArt Americana Colors: Country Blue DA41 (CB), Gooseberry Pink DA27 (GB), and Titanium White DA1 (TW)
- Two widths of flat brushes and a liner
- 14" length of ⅝"-wide ribbon for bow

For polka-dot basket
- DecoArt Americana Colors: Country Blue DA41 (CB)
- White 1"-diameter self-stick dots

For striped basket
- DecoArt Americana Colors: Gooseberry Pink DA27 (GB)
- White self-stick mailing labels
- Scallop-edge scissors

INSTRUCTIONS

Use a T-pin to make small holes in opposite sides of the box base about ⅜" below the top edge. Enlarge the holes with a nail to accommodate a chenille stem.

Base-coat all surfaces of the box base, using a large flat brush and

TW for the plaid basket, CB for the polka-dot basket, and GB for the striped basket. The lids will not be used for this project.

plaid basket

Add GB stripes to the basket sides, first painting horizontal stripes with the narrower flat brush and then painting vertical stripes with the wider flat brush. When the GB stripes are dry, use a liner brush to make fine CB lines in both directions on the basket.

polka-dot basket

Randomly press the 1"-diameter dots onto the basket sides. Trim off any part of the dots that extends beyond the top and bottom edges of the basket.

striped basket

Use scallop-edge scissors to finish the long edges of the mailing labels. Press the stripes evenly spaced on the basket sides, wrapping the stripes over the top edge and into the basket.

handle

Wrap the ribbon around a chenille stem so the ribbon stops ½" from the stem end; glue the ribbon ends to the stem. Insert the unwrapped stem ends into the holes in the basket; glue stem ends to inside of basket. Tie a bow with the ⅝"-wide ribbon around the handle of the plaid basket. ❤

Designer: Connie Matricardi
Photographer: Craig Anderson

waffle bowl may baskets

Shown *below* and on *page 89*.

MATERIALS

For one basket:
- Waffle bowl
- Toothpick
- Glitter stem or wired star garland
- Curling ribbons (optional)
- Colored plastic wrap (optional)
- Treats
- 4—4"-diameter paper lace doilies (optional)

INSTRUCTIONS

Use a toothpick to make small holes in opposite sides of the waffle bowl about ¾" below the top edge. Enlarge the holes with the toothpick to accommodate a wired garland or glitter stem.

For the handle, coil a length of star garland to measure about ¼". Insert ½" at the ends of the star garland or the glitter stem into the holes in the waffle bowl; fold ends up on the inside of bowl to secure the handle. Trim the handle with curling ribbon as desired.

If desired, wrap the treats in colored plastic wrap and tie with curling ribbon or star garland. If desired, line the bowl with doilies. Set the wrapped treats in the bowl. ❤

Designer: Laura Collins
Photographer: Perry Struse

star-and-stripes garments

Earrings measure 1¾" tall. Shown on *page 87*.

MATERIALS

For the sweatshirt

- Navy blue or red sweatshirt
- Water-soluble fabric marking pen
- Ruler and scissors or rotary cutter
- Red, white, and blue cotton embroidery floss
- Embroidery needle
- ⅓ yard of 17"-wide paper-backed fusible web
- 4" square of light print for star A
- 5" square of dark print for star B
- 2—4" squares of dark prints for stars C and D
- 3" square of light print for whirligig
- 3" square of dark print for whirligig

For the shortall

- Striped shortall
- Water-soluble fabric marking pen
- Red, white, and blue cotton embroidery floss
- Embroidery needle
- ⅓ yard of 17"-wide paper-backed fusible web
- 4" square of light print for star A
- 5" square of dark print for star B
- 2—4" squares of dark prints for stars C and D
- 2—3" squares of dark prints for whirligigs

For the earrings

- Scraps of two cotton print fabrics for front and backing
- Scrap of paper-backed fusible web
- Cotton embroidery floss
- Embroidery needle
- Liquid fabric stiffener
- Earring findings
- Glue gun and hotmelt adhesive

INSTRUCTIONS

sweatshirt

Wash and dry the sweatshirt before using fusible web.

Cut the lower hem band, wrist bands, and the neck band from the sweatshirt. Use a ruler and scissors or rotary cutter to straighten the cuff and the bottom edges.

To hem the bottom edge of the sweatshirt, fold and press 1" to the wrong side; pin. Make two rows of running stitches ¼" and ⅞" from the fold, using two strands of embroidery floss in a color that shows on the sweatshirt. Satin-stitch between the rows of running stitches, making groups of six stitches spaced 2" apart. Use four strands of floss for the satin stitches, changing the floss color after every two stitches. We satin stitched red, white, and blue on the navy sweatshirt and blue, white, and blue on the red sweatshirt.

To hem the sleeves, fold ½" toward the right side and pin. To hem the neck edge, fold ½" toward the wrong side and pin. Use two strands of floss to work running stitches ⅜" from the fold.

On the paper side of the fusible web, trace one of each star and two whirligigs from the patterns, *page 98*. Leave ½" between the shapes. Cut the shapes apart, leaving some excess web around each shape. Following the manufacturer's instructions, fuse

Continued

star-and-stripes garments

the shapes to the backs of the appropriate fabrics. Let the fabrics cool. Cut out the shapes on the traced lines, and remove paper.

Lay the sweatshirt, front side up, on a flat ironing surface. Referring to the photographs for placement, position star A, star B, star C, star D, and the light print whirligig on the sweatshirt; fuse. Lay the sweatshirt, back side up, on the ironing surface, and position the dark print whirligig on the center back about 2" below the neck edge; fuse.

Use two strands of floss to make running stitches on the stars ⅛" from the edges and down the center of the whirligigs. Referring to the photograph, use the water-soluble marking pen to draw a loosely looping line connecting the stars and whirligigs, being sure to continue the line over the shoulder to the back whirligig. Make running stitches on the marking pen lines, using two strands of floss in a color that shows on the sweatshirt.

shortall

Follow the instructions for the sweatshirt and refer to the photograph, *page 87*, for the placement of the shapes on the shortall. Blanket-stitch the top edge of the back pockets with two strands of red floss.

star earrings

On the paper side of the fusible web, trace one star. To reverse the star direction, trace one onto the adhesive side of the fusible web. Following the manufacturer's instructions, fuse the stars to the back of the print fabric selected for the front. Let the fabric cool. Cut out the stars on the traced lines, and remove paper backing. Fuse these stars to the wrong side of the remaining print fabric for backing.

Use two strands of floss to make running stitches on the stars ⅛" from the edges. Cut the backing fabric even with the edges of the stars. Following the manufacturer's instructions, stiffen the stars using the fabric stiffener. When the stars are completely dry, glue the earring findings to the back of the stars.💜

Designer: Jan Ballagh
Photographer: Craig Anderson

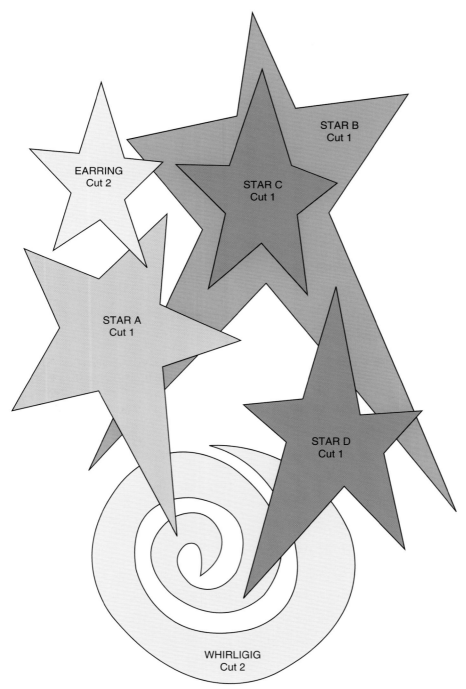

patriotic pots

Pots are 3¼", 4", and 5¾" tall.
Shown on *page 88–89.*

MATERIALS

- Tracing paper
- Graphite or transfer paper
- 3¼", 4", and 5¾" terra-cotta pots
- DecoArt Patio Paint Clear Coat DCP24
- Brushes: ½" and ¾" wash/glaze; #2, #10, and #12 flats; #2, #4, #8, and #12 shaders; ½" and ⅜" stipplers; 18/0 script liner; and a spatter brush or old toothbrush
- Toothpicks
- Fine-tip permanent black marking pen, such as Pigma .001

DecoArt Americana Colors

- AR Antique Rose DA156
- BC Black Green DA157
- BK Buttermilk DA3
- BL Blush Flesh DA110
- BS Burnt Sienna DA63
- CG Celery Green DA208
- DB Deep Burgundy DA128
- EG Evergreen DA82
- FF Light French Blue DA185
- KP Black Plum DA172
- LB Lamp Black DA67
- MF Medium Flesh DA102
- PG Payne's Grey DA167
- SA Sable Brown DA61
- TR True Ochre DA143
- UB Uniform Blue DA86

INSTRUCTIONS

prepare the pots

Wash each pot in warm, soapy water; rinse thoroughly, and let dry overnight. To seal the pots, apply one coat of Patio Paint Clear Coat to both the inside and outside surfaces of the pots; let the Clear Coat dry.

Trace the patterns, *page 101,* onto tracing paper; cut out, leaving a ¼" margin around the designs. Transfer the main design lines onto the pots with graphite paper. Don't transfer the details yet, you'll base-coat over them later.

paint the pots

Refer to the individual directions *below* for painting each pot and to the photograph, *above* and on *pages 88–89,* and patterns on *page 101,* as guides for shading and details. Base-coat the pots with wash, flat, or shader brushes, using a size that best fits the area. Use shader brushes to float shading. Dry-brush on highlights with a stippler. Apply details with the script liner brush. Use the handle end of a paintbrush or the tip of a toothpick to make dots.

firecracker pot

For the left firecracker, base-coat the top section DB; dry-brush with BL to highlight and shade with KP. Base-coat the center section BK; float SA

Continued

patriotic pots

shading on the outer edges. Base-coat the bottom section UB; dry-brush with FF to highlight and shade with PG. For the center section, paint the fine solid lines UB and the dashed lines DB.

Base-coat the middle firecracker DB. Dry-brush with BL to highlight. Use BK to paint fine vertical lines. Float KP shading along the edges of the firecracker.

For the right firecracker, base-coat alternating sections BK and UB. Shade and line the BK sections with SA. Dry-brush FF highlights on the UB sections. Apply DB dots to the UB sections. When the dots are dry, shade the UB sections with PG.

Use LB and the 18/0 liner brush to paint the wicks. Use BK to make dots spiraling out from the wicks and to make three-dot clusters randomly around the pot sides.

For the rim, paint the stars UB. Dry-brush FF highlights and shade the left side of the stars with PG. Apply DB dots between the stars.

watermelon pot

Base-coat the bird LB. Paint the beak and legs TR. Dot the eye BK. Base-coat the flag BK. Use DB and the 18/0 liner brush to paint the stripes. Paint the corner of the flag UB with a BK star. Paint the flag pole LB.

Base-coat the watermelon DB; dry-brush with BL to highlight. Float KP shading along the edges. Paint the seeds LB. Apply a small BK dot to the bottom right corner of each seed. Float KP shading on the left side of each seed. Paint a thin BK

line around the bottom of the watermelon for the inner rind. Paint an EG line around the bottom of the watermelon for the outer rind. Use EG and CG to paint double-dots around the side of the pot.

For the rim, use a #10 flat brush to paint alternating DB and EG squares. Use LB and the liner brush to outline the squares. Dry-brush BL highlights on the red squares and shade with KP. Dry-brush CG highlights on the green squares and shade with BC.

uncle sam pot

Base-coat the face MF; float BS shading on the face next to the hair and along the top of the nose. Blush the cheeks with AR. Dot the eyes LB. When the eyes are dry, add a tiny BK dot to each eye and the cheeks. Use BK and the liner brush to make some wispy bangs.

Base-coat the beard and mustache BK; float SA shading on the beard around the outer edges and under the mustache.

Base-coat the sleeves DB. Dry-brush with BL to highlight. Float KP shading on the sleeves along the bottom and next to the beard. Apply UB dots to the sleeves. Base-coat the hands MF; float BS shading on the hands next to the sleeves.

Base-coat the hat UB and dry-brush with FF to highlight. Float PG shading along the bottom of each hat section. Paint the hat band TR; float BS shading along the bottom edge.

Base-coat the flags BK; float SA shading along the edges. Paint the stripes DB and the corners of the

flags UB. Float PG shading around the edges of the blue corners. Paint the stars on the flags BK and the flag poles LB.

Paint BK stars randomly around the sides of the pot; apply a DB dot in the middle of each star.

For the rim, use a #12 flat brush to paint UB stripes. Dry-brush a FF highlight on the stripes. Float PG shading on the top and bottom edges of the stripes. Use a #2 flat brush to paint BK stripes between the wide blue stripes. Use a liner brush to make thin DB stripes on each side of the blue stripes.

finish the pots

Use the fine-tip permanent black marking pen to ink the details, referring to the photograph and patterns as guides.

Thin BK with water to ink consistency; dip a spatter brush or an old toothbrush into the diluted paint, and flick your thumb across the bristles to spatter the outside surface of each pot. Thin LB with water to ink consistency; spatter the outside surface of the Firecracker and Uncle Sam pots. Thin BC with water to ink consistency; spatter the outside surface of the watermelon pot.

When the paint is completely dry, apply a coat of Patio Paint Clear Coat to all surfaces of the pots. ♥

Designer: Myra Mahy
Photographer: Craig Anderson

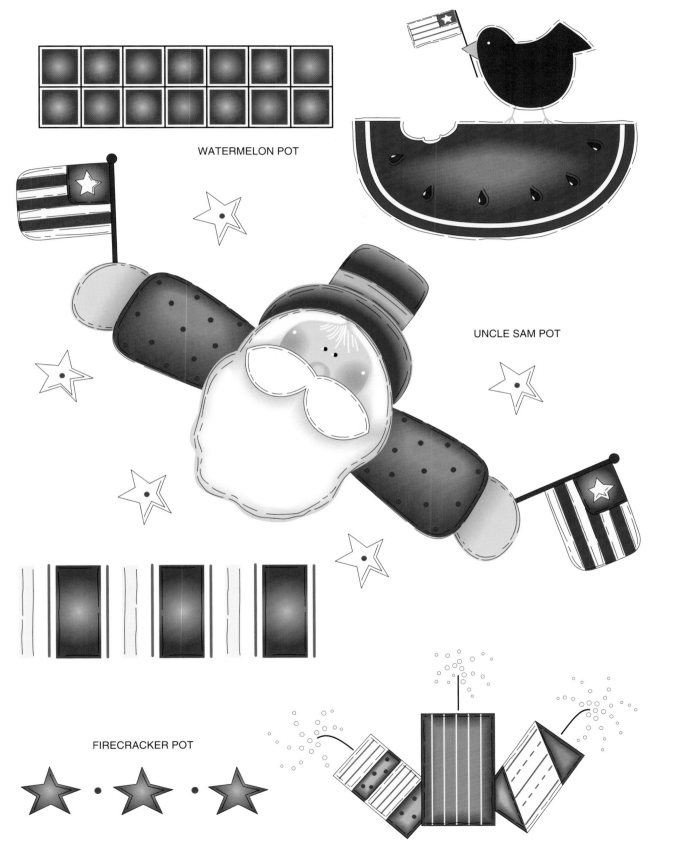

WATERMELON POT

UNCLE SAM POT

FIRECRACKER POT

jack-o'-lantern-in-the-house

House measures 17" tall. Shown at *right* and on *page 90*.

MATERIALS

- Tracing paper
- 4×4×14" papier-mâché box with lid
- Cardboard
- Black, dark gray, and orange construction paper
- ⅓ yard of orange knit fabric for body and head
- 2×30" strip of black print fabric for collar
- 2×30" strip of orange print fabric for collar trim
- 9×12" piece of black felt
- Corrugated wrapping paper
- Crafts glue
- Glue gun and hotmelt adhesive
- White acrylic paint
- Small sponge
- Colored pencils: red, orange, and green
- Fine-tip permanent black marking pen
- 2 small scraps of foam-core board
- 3"-wide flexible vinyl clothes dryer ducting
- Awl
- Masking tape
- Carpet thread
- 4"-diameter plastic foam ball
- 36" length of green tapestry yarn
- Large-eye needle
- Black raffia for hair
- 36" length of cord
- ½"-diameter wooden bead
- 18" length of 18-gauge florist's wire
- 3—1½"-diameter plastic spiders

INSTRUCTIONS

Trace the patterns, *pages 103–104*, onto tracing paper; cut out. Refer to the photographs as a guide for placement and details. Use crafts glue unless hot glue is specified.

cut the pieces

From cardboard, cut one 3¾" square base, one 2×10½" roof, one 1½×6¼" porch roof, one ½×6¼" left pillar, one ½×6" right pillar, one porch peak, six shutters, and one porch base. Score the roof 5" from one end; fold along score line. Score the porch roof 3½" from one end; fold along score line.

From black construction paper, cut three fences, four windowpanes, three hinges, one door handle, and three bats.

From dark gray construction paper, cut one door and three windows.

From orange construction paper, cut two tall pumpkins and one short pumpkin.

From orange knit fabric, cut one 10¾×20" rectangle (with the stretch lengthwise) for the body, and one 9" square for the head.

From black felt, cut one mouth, one nose, two eyes, and two eyebrows.

make the house

Glue corrugated wrapping paper on one surface of the roof, porch roof, left and right pillars, and shutters, positioning the paper so the ridges run lengthwise on the roofs and pillars and crosswise on the shutters. Trim the paper even with the cardboard edges. Use the sponge to lightly sponge white paint on the shutters.

Glue a windowpane to the back of the door and to the front of each window. Glue the door to the front of the box; glue hinges and the handle to the door. Glue a fence to each side and to the back of the box. Glue a window to each side and to the

front of the box. Glue the shutters to the box, positioning them slightly askew on the windows. Use a black marking pen to draw a spiderweb in the fence on each side of the house.

To construct the porch, cut the top of each pillar at an angle. Hot-glue the bottom of each pillar to the porch base as indicated by the lines on the pattern. Hot-glue the angled ends of the pillars to the porch roof, ¼" in from the front edge of roof. Use hot glue to attach the back edge of the porch base and the back edge of the porch roof to the front of the box.

Color the pumpkins with colored pencils to add dimension. Glue one tall pumpkin to the top of a back fence post. To make the pumpkins stand, glue a small piece of foam core to the bottom back of the two remaining pumpkins. Color the sides and back of the foam core with the black marking pen. Hot-glue the pumpkins to the porch base.

To hinge the roof, cut two parallel corners of the box lid from the bottom edge to the top of the lid. Center and make two holes ½" apart on the top of the lid, ⅜" in from the hinged edge. Place the lid on the box with the hinge to the back; hot-glue the hinge to the back of the box. Glue the roof peak to the front of the lid. Glue corrugated paper strips to all sides of the lid. Hot-glue the roof centered on the roof peak.

make the jack-o'-lantern

Draw a 3"-diameter circle centered on the 3¾" square cardboard base. Use an awl to punch pairs of holes through the base at each corner, making one on each side of the drawn circle. Count 50 rings of vinyl ducting; cut off the remainder of the ducting. Position the ducting over the drawn circle. Use a carpet-threaded needle to sew the bottom ring of the ducting to the base through the punched holes. Tie the thread ends together on the back of the base; masking tape the thread ends to the base.

For the body, sew together the long edges of the 10¾×20" orange knit rectangle, using a ⅜" seam allowance. Turn right side out and slip the fabric tube over the ducting. Use carpet thread to whipstitch the top edge of fabric to the top ring of the ducting. Glue the bottom edge of fabric to the base.

With right sides facing, sew the collar and collar trim strips together along one long edge, using ¼" seam allowances. Press the seam allowances toward the trim. Sew the short edges together, forming a circle. Press under ¼" on the remaining trim edge. Fold the trim in half with wrong sides together, covering the stitching; sew in place. Sew a row of gathering stitches ¼" from the raw edge of collar. Pull the threads, adjusting gathers evenly and easing the collar to fit around the top of the body. Hand-sew the collar to the inside of the top ring.

For the head, fold the 9" square of orange knit fabric in half with the stretch in the width; sew the long edges together. Turn the fabric tube right side out. With your hand, roll the plastic foam

ball on a hard surface to shape it into an oval. Slip the ball into the center of the fabric tube. Run a gathering thread around the bottom edge. Pull the thread snugly to bring the fabric together below the ball; knot thread. Hand-gather the fabric together at the top of the ball; secure with carpet thread. Tightly twist the excess fabric at the top into a stem and wrap the green tapestry wool around the stem. Secure the end of the wool by threading the yarn through a needle and inserting the needle back down through the stem. Cut off excess wool and fabric.

Glue the mouth, nose, eyes, and eyebrows to the front of head. Tie a bunch of raffia around the base of stem for hair. Set head aside.

finish the house

Slip the bead onto the cord and thread each cord end through a hole in the lid, going from the top of the lid to inside the box. Knot the two cord ends together. Hot-glue the base to the inside bottom of the box with the seam in the fabric body at the back

Pull the cord attached to the top of this spooky little house. The whole roof folds back to reveal a jack-o'-lantern.

of the box. Let the glue set. Pull the fabric-covered ducting up and out of the box as far as it will go. Pin the knot at the ends of the cord to the center back of the ducting, as far down as possible; sew the knot securely to the ducting.

Hot-glue the head to the top of the body. Push the head and body down inside the box and close lid. Adjust the bead on the cord, and make a knot in the cord above the bead. Pull the cord to open lid and pull the jack-o'-lantern out.

Cut the florist's wire into two unequal pieces. Glue a bat to one end of each wire. Slip the other ends of the wires behind the porch roof; hot-glue them to the box. Glue the remaining bat to the front of the roof peak. Randomly glue the spiders to the house. ♥

Designer: Phyllis Dunstan
Photographer: Craig Anderson

Full-size patterns for the house are on page 104.

FACE PIECES
Cut 1 Each

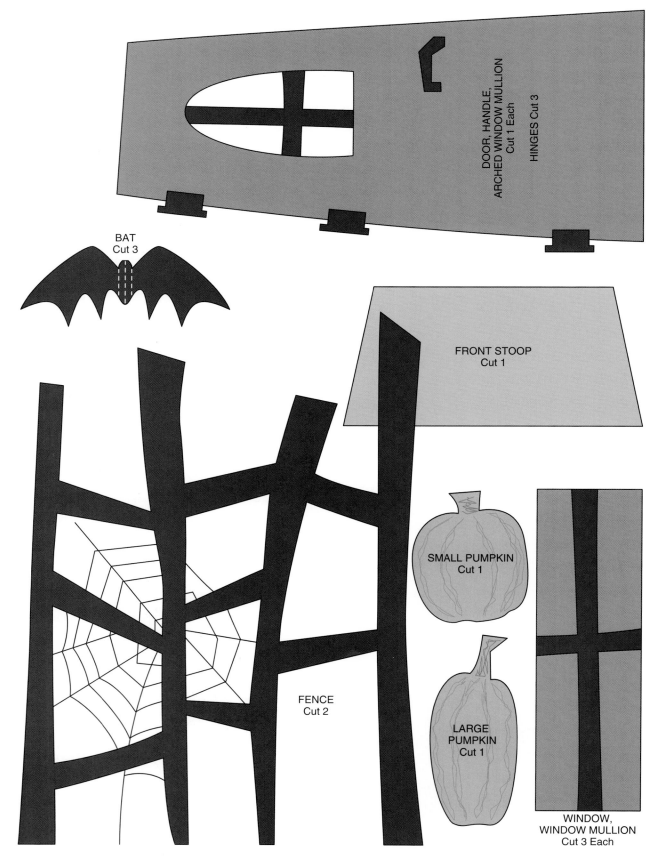

DOOR, HANDLE,
ARCHED WINDOW MULLION
Cut 1 Each

HINGES Cut 3

BAT
Cut 3

FRONT STOOP
Cut 1

SMALL PUMPKIN
Cut 1

FENCE
Cut 2

LARGE
PUMPKIN
Cut 1

WINDOW,
WINDOW MULLION
Cut 3 Each

fall goodie box

Shown *above* and on *page 90*.

MATERIALS

- Tracing paper
- Graphite paper
- 8×4½×1¾" Cabin Crafters wooden box with lower lip
- Acrylic matte sealer/finish
- Black permanent ink pen
- 16 gauge wire
- E6000 glue or epoxy
- Raffia
- Brushes: ¾" glaze/wash; #12, #6, and #2 flat; ½" angular shader; and #1 liner

Delta Ceramcoat Colors

- AG Dark Goldenrod 2519
- BU Burnt Umber 2025
- BY Butter Yellow 2102
- FG Forest Green 2010
- LE Leprechaun 2422
- LI Light Ivory 2401
- NW Napa Wine 2443
- TC Terra Cotta 2081
- TF Toffee Brown 2086
- TR Trail Tan 2435

INSTRUCTIONS

Drill a hole in each end of the box. Base-coat the bottom of the box with FG, the fronts and sides with TR; the top edge of the box with LI. Trace the outlines of the pattern onto tracing paper. Use graphite paper to transfer to the box.

Paint alternating checks near the top of the box NW, TC, and LE. Shade with BU. Base-coat the pumpkins with TC and shade with BU. Dry-brush highlights with AG. Basecoat the stem TF and shade with BU. Paint the leaves with LE and shade with FG. Paint the candy corn with stripes of LI, TC, and BY. Shade with BU. Paint the stars LI and BY.

Outline and add all details with black permanent ink pen. Add wire handle. Spray with several coats of sealer/finisher. Add raffia bow.❤

Designer: Laurie Speltz
Photographer: Craig Anderson

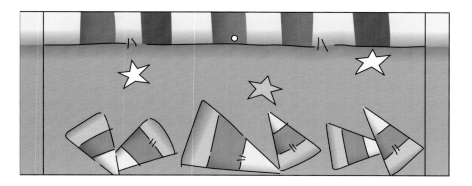

place card treats

Triangle box is 5×1¾ long". Cone measures 8" long. Shown *above* and on *page 91*.

MATERIALS

For the triangle place card
- Stamp Your Art Out triangle box template
- 1 sheet of decorative paper
- Lightweight cardboard and glue (opt.)
- 3 sheets of fall-colored papers
- Marvy 2" maple leaf paper punch
- Double-stick tape
- Foam tape
- Marvy gold pen

For the leaf cone
- 3 sheets of fall-colored card stock
- Mrs. Grossman Paper Whispers Fall Leaf stickers
- Fiskars Ripple paper edgers
- Marvy gold pen
- Double-stick tape
- Scissors

INSTRUCTIONS

triangle place card
Use a pencil to trace the box template onto the wrong side of the decorative paper; cut out on traced lines. For a sturdier box, glue the decorative paper onto lightweight cardboard, trace the template, and cut out. Fold the box and secure with double-stick tape.

For the name tag, cut 4½×1¾" and 4¼×1½" rectangles from two colored papers. Layer the name tag rectangles with double-stick tape; tape to the front of the box. Use the maple leaf punch to punch out one leaf from two colored papers. Use foam tape to layer the leaves on the top left corner of the box. Personalize the name tag with the gold pen.

leaf cone
For the cone, cut a 7½" square from one sheet of card stock. Fold the square into a cone, bringing the sides inward to overlap approximately 2½". If necessary, crease the paper at the cone bottom to aid in folding. Use double-stick tape to secure. Trim the open end so the cone is approximately 7½" long.

Cut a 2½"- and a 3"-wide strip from the remaining sheets of card stock. Use the ripple paper edges to finish one long edge of each strip. Layer the strips with double-stick tape, aligning the straight long edges. Tape the strips around the open end of the cone so they extend about ½" from the cone. Press leaf stickers onto the cone close to the edge. Cut around each leaf closely. Use the gold pen to make dots around the leaves.❤

Designer: Suzanne State
Photographer: Craig Anderson

maple leaf favor

Bag is 5½" tall, excluding the handles. Shown on *page 93*.

MATERIALS
- 1 sheet of ivory card stock
- Small brown handled sack
- PSX maple leaf stamp #B1077
- Printworks ink pads: Peacock Blue, Truffle Brown, and Vintage Wine
- Marvy burgundy and gold metallic pens
- 3¼×1¾" rectangle of burgundy card stock
- Foam tape

INSTRUCTIONS
From the ivory card stock, cut a 6"-square leaf collar and a 2¾×1¼" rectangular name tag. Use a pencil to lightly draw a 6"-diameter circle on the card stock square to use as a guide for leaf placement. Fold the square in half; cut a slit along the fold to accommodate the handles.

Using all colors of ink pads, stamp the maple leaf randomly on the front of the sack and around the circle on the card stock square. Stamp one leaf on a scrap. Use the gold metallic pen to outline the leaves on the collar and the scrap. Cut out the single leaf. Cut around the outside of the leaf circle.

Use the burgundy pen to personalize the name tag; draw a gold metallic dashed line ⅛" from the tag edges. Use foam tape to tape the single leaf on the name tag, the name tag on the burgundy rectangle, and the burgundy rectangle on the front of the collar. Slip the collar over the bag handles.

Designer: Suzanne State
Photographer: Perry Struse

floral horn of plenty

Cornucopia measures 36".
Shown on *page 92*.

MATERIALS
- Cornucopia basket
- Florist's foam
- Glue gun and hotmelt adhesive
- Spanish moss
- Greening pins
- One bunch of dried wheat
- 12 stems of assorted fall-colored silk flowers
- Assorted fruits and vegetables
- 18-gauge floral wire
- Wire clippers
- Florist's tape
- 5 stems of berries
- 1 bunch of dried billy balls

INSTRUCTIONS
Cut a block of florist's foam to fit into the bottom of the cornucopia basket. Hot-glue the foam inside the basket; let the glue set. Cover the foam with Spanish moss, using greening pins to secure.

To arrange the basket, visualize an invisible line down the center. Use the left side mainly for dried wheat and silk flowers and the right side mainly for fruits and vegetables.

Start the arrangement at the bottom with the dried wheat. Divide the wheat bunch in half; set one half aside. Cut the remaining half at different lengths; glue it to the foam on the left side of the basket.

Continue to fill the cornucopia with silk flowers, fruits, and vegetables, mixing the textures and changing the height of the elements. Be sure to use the leaves and flower buds in your arrangement. Use 18-gauge wire to anchor the fruits and vegetables at different angles, wrapping the wire with florist's tape. When you have used most of the elements, cross over the invisible line with the flowers and the fruits and vegetables.

When you are satisfied with the position of the flowers, fruits, and vegetables, fill in any large gaps with more silk and dried flowers. Fill the small gaps with the dried billy balls and the berry stems. ❤

Designer: Lenny Houts
Photographer: Scott Little

easy patchwork table runner

Table runner is 27×63". Shown on *page 92–93*.

MATERIALS
- ⅓ yard of dark red print
- ⅓ yard of tan print
- Scraps of prints, plaids, and stripes in assorted colors (red, rust, brown, tan, gray, green, gold)
- 1½ yards of orange print for border
- 5 yards of wide red rickrack
- 1⅞ yards of backing fabric
- 30×66" of quilt batting

INSTRUCTIONS
All fabrics are 44/45" wide. Measurements have been adjusted to allow for shrinkage. All seam allowances are ¼".

cut the fabrics
To make the best use of your fabrics, cut the pieces in the order that follows. Cut strips across the width of the fabric. For this project, cut the border strips lengthwise (parallel to the selvage). The measurements given are mathematically correct. You may wish to add extra length now to allow for possible sewing differences.

From dark red print, cut:
- 3—3½×42" strips. Cut one strip in half to make two 3½×21" strips.

From tan print, cut:
- 3—3½×42" strips Cut one strip in half to make two 3½×21" strips.

From assorted scraps, cut:
- 84—2" squares

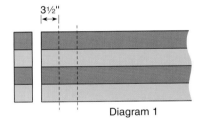

Diagram 1

From orange print, cut:
- 2—6½×51½" border strips
- 2—6½×27½" border strips

center
Aligning the long edges, sew the dark red print 3½×42" strips to the tan 3½×42" strips alternately to make a strip set (see Diagram 1). Press the seam allowance toward the red strips. Repeat with the 3½×21" strips. From the two strip sets, cut a total of 16—3½" wide segments.

Lay out the strip set segments, alternating the red and tan squares (see photograph) to form a checkerboard pattern. Sew together the segments. Press the seam allowances in one direction.

inner border

Sew together 32 assorted print 2" squares to make a long pieced inner border. Press the seam allowances in one direction. Repeat to make another long pieced border. Sew borders to the long sides of the center. Press the seam allowances toward the center.

Sew together 10 assorted print 10" squares to make pieced inner border. Repeat. Sew these borders to the ends of the center. Press the seam allowances toward the center.

outer border

Sew one orange print 6½×51½" border to each long side of the pieced center. Then add a 6½×27½" border to each end. Press all seam allowances toward the outer border.

finish

Sew the rickrack to the right side of the raw edges of the table runner. Layer the table runner top, batting, and backing. Quilt as desired. This table runner was machine-quilted diagonally through the center squares, outlined around the inner pieced border, and in parallel lines about ½" apart in the outer border.

When quilting is complete, trim the backing and batting even with the raw edge of the table runner top. Trim an additional ½" of batting. Fold the raw edges of the top layer to the inside along the rickrack sew line. Turn under ½" of backing and blindstitch folded edge to rickrack. ♥

Designer: Jim Williams
Photographers: Marcia Cameron and Scott Little

snowy winter night

Shown on *page 94.*

MATERIALS
- ½×8×15" piece of wood
- 3 tablespoons
- 18" rag strip hanger
- Three 13" rag strips
- Sanding pad
- 14 decorative upholstery tacks
- 4 felt pads
- Brown antiquing gel
- Metal primer
- Interior/exterior varnish
- Brushes: #1 and #10 stiff bristle; #4 and #8 shader; #1 liner; ¾" flat

Delta Ceramcoat Colors
-     Black 2506
- AU Dark Burnt Umber 2527
- BS Burnt Sienna 2030
- BU Burnt Umber 2025
- CY Cayenne 2428
- DN Dark Night Blue 2414
- DS Desert Sun Orange 2444
- GB Golden Brown 2054
- LC Lichen Grey 2118
- LI Light Ivory 2401
- NF Nightfall Blue 2131
- OW Oyster White 2492
- SG Stonewedge Green 2442
- TB Territorial Beige 2425
- WG Wedgwood Green 2070
- WM Williamsburg Blue 2524

INSTRUCTIONS

plaque preparation

Sand the wood as needed. Apply one coat of sealer and let it dry. Base-coat front, back, and sides of wood DN. Trace the pattern on *page 111,* and use graphite paper to transfer portions as directed

snow

Transfer the horizon line between sky and ground. Base-coat all of the snow LI. When base coat is dry, transfer lines for hills and shade behind them DN using a ¾" flat brush. Transfer snowman, cat, moon, and two tall tree shapes. Dry-brush DN under snowman, cat, and two tall trees with a #1 stiff bristle brush.

sky

Dry-brush NF on the moon and the sky around the snowman and tall trees. Dry-brush with WM between the moon, snowman, and trees, leaving some of the darker background showing around each figure, using a #10 stiff bristle brush.

Thin LI with water and paint the entire moon (you'll be able to clearly see the dark blue sky through the

Continued

snowy winter night

moon). Let dry. Paint again, using a "pit-patting" motion with your brush to get a mottled effect. If you want to deepen the color, add a third coat or just "pit-pat" thinned paint in specific areas. Spatter "snow" in sky with LI. Let dry completely. Using a ¾" flat brush, shade the left/top side of the moon with LC, lifting and patting your brush and walking it out toward the center of the moon as you go along, so you get a mottled shading; shade those same areas BU, but don't walk it out so far into the center; finish with a shading of AU around the edges of those same areas.

fence

Transfer fence and paint black. On the upper row of fencing, paint LI snow on top of rails.

snowman

Paint head and body of snowman NF. Transfer the line that separates the body sections. For the head and body, use a large shader to "pit-pat" OW on the snowman, leaving it sparse along edges and in the shadows, and building up a deeper color toward the centers and right side of each section. Shade the snowman as you did the moon, first with LC, then BU, and finally AU. When dry, transfer snowman details. Dry brush cheeks CY. Paint eyes, mouth, and buttons black. Shade to the left of each button BU. Paint twig arms TB; shade with BU and then lightly outline along left and bottom with AU. Paint hat and scarf CY, leaving a thin line of blue background showing where sections meet. Shade left and bottom with BS, then AU. Float DS on the right side of the hat and scarf to highlight them. Paint candle WG. Shade left side BU and outline with SG on the right side.

Continued on page 112.

snowy winter night

Continued from page 110.

Paint the candleholder black. Use a dry brush to paint a LI highlight on the holder. Paint flame CY; paint GB on the right side of the flame and WM on the bottom.

cat

Paint cat black. When dry, transfer white areas, legs, and tail. Paint those areas LI, leaving a thin line of black showing through where white colors meet each other. Shade the black and white areas with LC. Transfer facial details. Thin black and paint eyes, nose, and mouth. Paint scarf WG. Shade with BU, then AU. Use a dry brush to paint SG highlights.

trees

Paint the tree trunks TB. Shade side away from the moon BU, then AU. Stroke LI highlights on side facing moon with a dry brush. Shade DN under each trunk. Use #1 stiff bristle brush to stipple all foliage AU. Stipple the foliage that faces the moon SG, and the foliage that faces away from the moon GB, allowing some of the AU to show through.

border

Transfer border and paint SG. When dry, transfer design to each corner. Use a #1 liner to paint the corner designs and the thin border black.

plaque finishing

Sand the edges of the plaque. Apply a light coat of brown antiquing gel with a very damp paper towel, staining mostly sanded edges rather than the design itself. Mark positions for two upholstery tack on each side and five

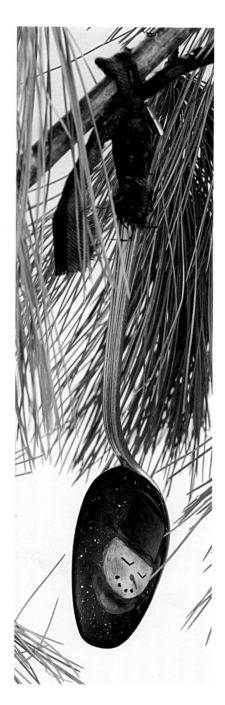

spoon preparation

Paint the front and back of each spoon bowl with metal primer and let dry. Because it is difficult to transfer designs to the bowl of a spoon, you may prefer to use the pattern as a guide and draw the designs free-hand.

green spoon

Paint the bowl SG. When dry, paint design black.

blue spoons

Paint the bowls DN; let dry. Dry-brush the inner bowl with NF, then a smaller section WM. Spatter lightly with LI. When dry, paint the designs, following plaque instructions.

spoon finishing

Paint a Black border around the edge of each spoon bowl. When dry, apply two coats of varnish to the front and back of the bowl section. Tie a rag strip around each handle and hang.❤

Designer: Donna Atkins
Photographer: Craig Anderson

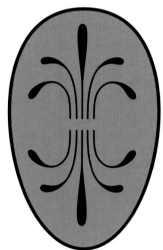

across the top and bottom. Push in the upholstery tacks, leaving a little gap between the tack head and the wood. Staple the 18" rag strip to the back of the plaque and attach the a felt pad to each back corner.

heart mittens

Shown *right* and on *page 95*.

MATERIALS

- One set of four or five size 4 double-pointed knitting needles, or size to obtain gauge
- 100 g. of red worsted-weight yarn
- 50 g. of natural worsted-weight yarn
- Three ring markers
- One safety pin for the stitch holder
- Yarn needle

Gauge: In St st and color pat, 26 sts and 28 rows=4"

Knitting terms
beg—beginning
bet—between
CO—cast on
cont—continue
dec—decrease
dpn—double-pointed needles
est—established
inc—increase
k—knit
p—purl
pat—pattern
pm—place marker
psso—pass slipped st over
rem—remain(ing)
rep—repeat
rnd—round
RS—right side
sl—slip
st(s)—stitch(es)
tog—together
WS—wrong side

INSTRUCTIONS

When using four dpn, place the 23 stitches for the back of the hand (the side opposite the thumb) on one needle, and divide the rem sts over the other two needles. When using five dpn, divide the sts evenly over four dpn.

When working the color pat, pick up the new color from under the previous color, and twist it over the previous color to prevent a hole. Carry the unused color loosely across the WS, catching it in the work every 3 to 4 sts.

right mitten–cuff

With red yarn, CO 48 sts and divide over the dpn. Take care not to twist the sts on the first rnd. Place a marker for the join at the beg of rnd.

Rnds 1–30 (RS): * K 2, p 2; rep from * around.

Rnd 31: K and inc 4 sts evenly around for a total of 52 sts.

hand section

Reading Chart 1, *opposite*, from right to left, beg with Rnd 1 and k 3 sts, pm, k 3 sts, pm, complete rnd. K every rnd through Rnd 7, end at the joining marker.

Rnd 8 (Beg thumb gusset): K 3 sts, work Rnd 1 of Chart 2 bet markers as follows: inc in next st, k1, inc in next st; complete Rnd 8 of Chart 1—54 sts.

K 2 rnds more, working Chart 2 between the gusset markers; end at the joining marker.

Rnd 11: K 3 sts, work Rnd 4 of Chart 2 bet the markers as follows: inc in next st, k 3, inc in next st; complete Rnd 11 of Chart 1—56 sts.

Rnds 12–19: Cont in est pat, working the thumb gusset as shown

on Chart 2 across the sts bet the gusset markers and working incs twice more—60 sts.

Rnd 20: K 2 sts, remove markers and sl next 13 sts (11 gusset sts plus 1 solid st each side) to a safety pin; CO 5 sts with red, complete Rnd 20—52 sts. Work through Rnd 46 of Chart 1, pm after first 26 sts to mark the center point.

Rnd 47 (dec rnd): * K1, sl 1, k1, psso, k to 3 sts before the next marker, k 2 tog; rep from * once to complete the rnd—48 sts. Work to the top of the chart and rep the dec rnd as indicated on the chart until 16 sts rem. Cut both of the yarns. Thread the red yarn tail through a yarn needle. Weave the tail through the rem sts and pull tightly to close the tip. Weave in both of the yarn tails on the WS. Use the tapestry needle to weave any other yarn tails into the the WS.

thumb
Sl 13 sts from safety pin back to two dpn; with third dpn and red yarn, pick up and k 9 sts on the CO edge opposite the gusset—22 sts. Complete the thumb following Rnds 13-30 of Chart 2, shaping the sides where indicated on the chart using the same method as given for the hand. Finish off in the same manner as the hand.

left mitten
Work the cuff in the same manner as for the first mitten. For the hand section, work in the same manner as the right mitten, but follow Charts 1 from the left to the right to reverse the pattern placement. ♥

Designer: Jean LemMon
Photographer: Perry Struse

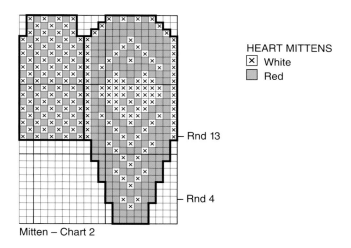

Mitten – Chart 2

HEART MITTENS
☒ White
▨ Red

Rnd 13
Rnd 4

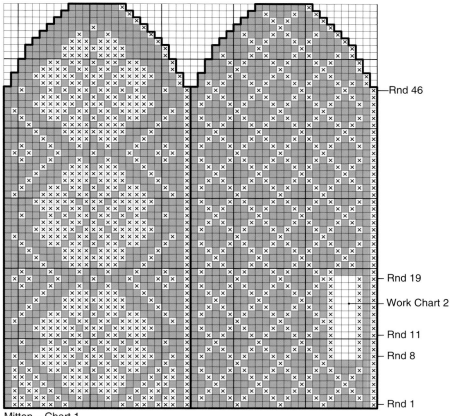

Mitten – Chart 1

Rnd 46
Rnd 19
Work Chart 2
Rnd 11
Rnd 8
Rnd 1

Model Magic Pens
start on *page 123.*

Drawer Organizer
starts on *page 123.*

Teacher's Mug
starts on *page 124.*

MAKING THE
grade

How do you teach *teachers* that
they're terrific? Create personal and handmade
gifts—even better, involve your child.

Have your child *decorate* a plastic desk-organizer
tray with stickers, and fill it with all kinds of snacks
and teacher-usable things, *left.* A student can
also create a one-of-a-kind *pen* by covering
a plain one in modeling compound and pushing
cool stuff into it, *left.* Or, give the child a set
of paint pens for *personalizing* a mug that
doubles as a pencil holder, *left.*

Teacher Votive Holder starts on *page 124*.

Coach's Clipboard starts on *page 127*.

In school or out, it's easy to remember the *coach*. Lay a clear plastic clipboard over the patterns, and trace the simple patterns (or make up your own). Then ask *team* members to add their names.

No doubt about it, this gift rates an $A+$. The painted teacher votive, *left,* is an *ingenious* combination of precut wood shapes, wood accessories, and plenty of attention to detail. Note the matchstick "chalk" and blackboard in the teacher's hands and the cutout that holds the lighted *votive*.

**Apple Box
starts on *page 121*.**

Give an appreciated teacher more than one *apple*—give her a
whole *tree* to enjoy for many years to come. You can paint it
in apple-pie order, starting with a preassembled box, full-size patterns,
and complete painting instructions.

apple box

Box measures 4⅝×9⅞×12⅜".
Shown *opposite*.

MATERIALS
- Graphite paper
- Purchased planter box
- Wood sealer
- Brushes: #2, #4, #8, and #12 flat; ⅜" angular shader; #1 round; #1 liner; small scruffy flat; and spatter brush or old toothbrush
- Krylon 1311 Matte-Finish Spray

DecoArt Americana Colors
- AM   Antique Maroon DA160
- AV   Avocado DA52
- BK   Buttermilk DA3
- CE   Cherry Red DA159
- DW   Driftwood DA171
- LB   Lamp Black DA67
- PP   Plantation Pine DA113
- RW   Raw Umber DA130

INSTRUCTIONS
Sand all surfaces of the box with medium- and then fine-grit sandpaper. Remove the sanding dust with a tack cloth. Apply wood sealer to all surfaces, and let the sealer dry. Sand again with fine-grit sandpaper, and wipe clean with a tack cloth.

Refer to the photograph, *opposite,* and patterns, *below* and on *page 122,* as guides for shading, highlighting, and details. Base-coat with the flat brushes, using the size that best fits the area. Float shading with a ⅜" angular shader brush. Paint small areas with a #1 round brush, and apply details with a #1 liner brush. Dry-brush highlights with a small scruffy flat brush.

Base-coat the front of the box and the front of the back piece DW. Transfer or measure and mark a ½"-wide border on the sides and bottom of the front piece. Paint the border and the remainder of the box AM. Let the paint dry thoroughly. For a worn look, sand paint randomly to reveal the wood grain; sand harder to remove more paint from the edges. Use graphite paper to transfer the main pattern lines to the front of the box and to the front of the back piece.

front section
Use the chisel edge of a #8 flat brush and RW to paint the ground area. The color should get lighter as it comes toward the bottom of the box. Repeat to deepen the color under the various objects.

Base-coat the wheelbarrow box RW. Mix RW and LB 1:1; use this mixture to shade the wheelbarrow box and to paint the wheel, spokes, and supports. Highlight all parts of the wheelbarrow with floated DW as shown on the pattern. Dot the nails RW. Mix RW and BK 1:1; use this mixture to highlight the nails.

Paint the apples and the leaves the same as on the back section. Paint the stems RW. Mix equal parts of RW and BK; use this mixture to highlight the stems. Base-coat the apple core BK, and shade with DW. Paint the ends of the apple core CE.

back section
You will find it easier to paint the back if you turn the box upside down with the top edge facing you. Base-coat the tree trunk, the limbs, and the stems RW. Let the paint dry, then dry-brush DW highlights on the trunk and limbs as shown on the pattern. Using a #1 round brush, base-coat the leaves AV. Float PP shading on the lower side of each leaf. Mix equal parts of AV and DW, dilute the mixture with water to ink

Continued

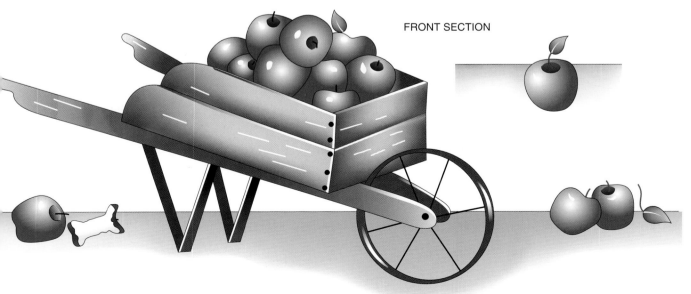

FRONT SECTION

apple box

BACK SECTION
Half pattern

A

Match
A to B

consistency; use a #1 liner brush and the diluted mixture to paint the vein lines.

Base-coat the apples CE, and shade with AM. Dry-brush a BK highlight on the edge of each apple. Paint a small BK stroke over the dry-brushed area for a stronger highlight.

finish the box

Spray all surfaces of the box with Krylon 1311 Matte-Finish Spray. Dilute LB with water to ink consistency. Dip a spatter brush or an old toothbrush into the diluted paint, and spatter all surfaces of the box. Let the paint dry. Spray again with Krylon 1311 Matte-Finish Spray.❤

Designer: Nelda Rice
Photographer: Perry Struse

Match
A to B

B

model magic pens

Pens measure about 6½" long.
Shown *below* and on *pages 116–117*.

MATERIALS

- Stick-style ballpoint pens
- Assorted colors of Crayola Model Magic modeling compound
- Small items to press into the modeling compound, such as beads, buttons, charms, bells, paper clips, fine wire, and toolbox items
- Ribbon and ribbon rose for white pen
- Crafts glue

INSTRUCTIONS

Press modeling compound around the pen in the desired shape, then push assorted small items into the compound. For the yellow pen, thread beads and bells onto fine wire; push the wire ends into the top of pen. Let the compound dry.

For the white pen, tie ribbon into a bow around the pen and glue a ribbon rose to the center of the bow. If items are loose after the compound dries, glue them in place.❤

Designer: Laura Collins
Photographer: Craig Anderson

drawer organizer

Tray measures 9×14".
Shown *above* and on *page 116*.

MATERIALS

- 9×14" clear plastic drawer-organizer tray
- Assorted stickers, including alphabet stickers
- Items to fill the tray compartments, such as colored pens, markers, pencils, erasers, wrapped candies, tea bags, self-adhesive notes, stickers, rubber bands, paper clips, and brass brads
- Assorted grosgrain ribbons

INSTRUCTIONS

Use stickers to decorate the compartments and the sides of the tray. Fill the tray with useful, colorful items. Use the top self-adhesive note for the gift tag. Wrap ribbon around some of the items and tie in bows.❤

Designer: Laura Collins
Photographer: Craig Anderson

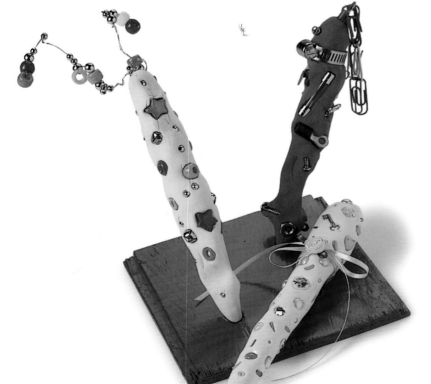

teacher's mug

Shown *above* and on *page 116–117.*

MATERIALS
- Tracing paper and masking tape
- 10×14" clear acrylic mug
- Red, white, blue, green, yellow, orange, white, brown, and black permanent paint pens

INSTRUCTIONS
Wash the mug in warm, soapy water, removing any fingerprints; rinse and dry well. Trace the pattern, *below,* onto tracing paper; cut out, leaving a ⅛" margin. Position and tape the tracing inside the mug.

Use black paint pen for "Teacher" and school colors to outline each letter. Highlight with white dots. Use black for the checkerboard on the left side. Use red for the apple. Add a white highlight, brown stem, and green leaf. Use yellow, blue, and white to add small dots randomly to the rest of the mug. ❤

Designer: Cut-It-Up
Photographer: Craig Anderson

teacher votive holder

Candleholder measures 5" tall.
Shown *opposite* and on *page 118.*

MATERIALS
- Tracing paper
- Graphite or transfer paper
- 1×3⅝×5¼" piece of pine for book
- ½×4×5" piece of Baltic birch plywood for teacher
- ⅛×¾×1⅛" piece of Baltic birch plywood for chalkboard
- 1" length of ³⁄₁₆" dowel
- Scrollsaw
- Router
- Drill; 2", ³⁄₁₆", ⁵⁄₃₂" drill bits
- Medium- and fine-grit sandpaper
- Tack cloth
- Wood sealer
- Toothpicks
- Fine-tip permanent black marking pen
- 5-minute epoxy
- Wooden match
- Votive cup and candle
- Brushes: #4, #6, and #8 flat and #00 liner

Delta Ceramcoat Colors
- AC   AC Flesh 2085
- AW   Antique White 2001
- •   Black 2506
- BI   Brown Iron Oxide 2023
- BJ   Blue Jay 2059
- BS   Burnt Sienna 2030
- CM   Cinnamon 2495

- DG   Dark Goldenrod 2519
- FG   Forest Green 2010
- MO   Mocha Brown 2050
- MS   Maple Sugar Tan 2062
- NF   Nightfall Blue 2131
- RO   Rouge 2404
- TF   Toffee Brown 2086
- WM   Williamsburg Blue 2524

INSTRUCTIONS

Trace the teacher pattern, *page 126,* onto tracing paper. Use graphite paper to transfer the outline of the teacher onto the ½" Baltic birch plywood. Cut out the shape with a scrollsaw. For the book, use the router to round one 5¼" edge for the spine and to cut out a ½"-wide strip from the remaining edges for the pages. Drill ³⁄₁₆" holes, ½" deep, in the book and in the bottom of the teacher as indicated on the patterns, *page 126.* Drill a ⁵⁄₃₂" hole, ⅜" deep, in the teacher's hand for the match. Use the 2" drill bit to make a ⅛"- to ¼"-deep recessed area in the book for the candle cup.

Sand all surfaces of the pieces with medium- and then fine-grit sandpaper. Remove the sanding dust with a tack cloth. Apply wood sealer to all surfaces, and let the sealer dry. Lightly sand again with fine-grit sandpaper, and wipe clean with a tack cloth.

paint the pieces

Refer to the photograph, *right,* and patterns as guides for placement, shading, and details. Base-coat with flat brushes, using the size that best fits the area. Use a side-loaded flat brush to shade and highlight. Apply details with the liner brush. Use the handle end of a paintbrush or the tip of a toothpick to make dots. Avoid painting areas where they'll be joined later, as epoxy does not bond permanently to painted surfaces.

Transfer the main design lines onto the teacher with graphite paper. Don't

transfer the details yet, you'll base-coat over them. Base-coat all surfaces of the pieces, continuing the design onto the back of the pieces.

Base-coat the face and hands MS. Use a wash of BS to paint the hair. Base-coat the outer and upper areas of sleeves and along the lower edge of the dress RO. While RO is still wet, base-coat the remaining areas of the sleeves and the lower dress CM; blend paints together. Base-coat the apron AC. Base-coat the chalkboard black and the frame MO. Base-coat the book cover WM and the pages AC.

When the paint is completely dry, sand the pieces with a paper grocery sack to remove the wood grain raised

by the paint. Remove the sanding dust with a tack cloth. Paint the details freehand, or if desired, transfer the details to the wood pieces with graphite paper.

Float BS shading on the face along the neck and hair edges and on the hands along the sleeves. Dot the eyes with black. When the eyes are dry, add a tiny BJ dot to the bottom right corners. Mix MS and BS ratio; use mixture to dot the nose. Use CM to dot the mouth and to very lightly blush the cheeks.

Float BI shading on the lower edge of the hair bun and on the hair next

Continued

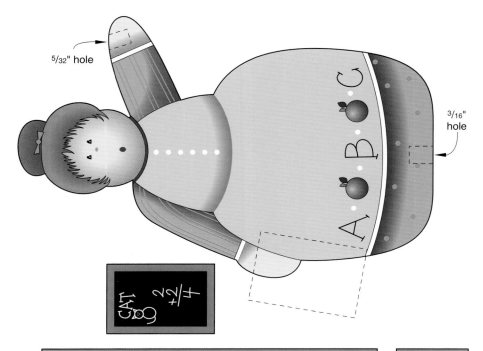

5/32" hole

3/16" hole

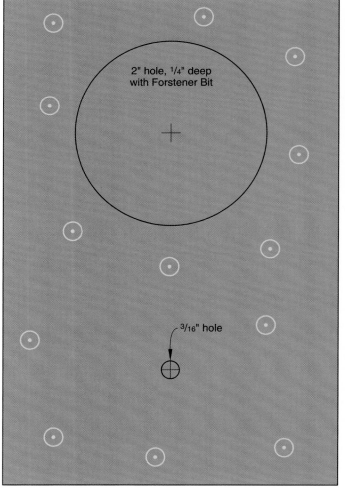

2" hole, 1/4" deep
with Forstener Bit

3/16" hole

ABC

teacher votive holder

to the face. Use the liner and BI to paint the hair wisps. Paint a tiny BJ bow at the bottom of the bun.

Use BJ to paint the fine lines on the sleeves and to dot the lower dress. Float TF shading on the upper apron next to the waist. Use the liner brush and AW to paint the thin line at the bottom of the apron and each sleeve. Dot the buttons AW. Use the liner and CM to outline the neckline of the apron. Use the fine-tip black permanent marking pen to write "ABC" along the bottom of the apron. Paint the apples CM; add a RO highlight on the top of the apples. Paint the leaves FG and the stems MO. Make AW dots between the letters and apples.

Thin AW with water to ink consistency; use the diluted paint to add the lettering, math problem, and drawing on the chalkboard.

Float TF shading along the edges of the book pages. Use NF to paint the label on the book's spine. Use the liner brush to paint fine DG and AC lines on each side of the label. Use AC to paint "ABC" on the label and to randomly make circles with dots on the book cover.

finish the votive holder

Epoxy the chalkboard to the teacher's hand. Glue the match in the hole at the end of the outstretched arm. Apply glue to both ends of the dowel; use the dowel to glue the teacher to the book.♥

Designer: Sue Jernigan
Photographer: Perry Struse

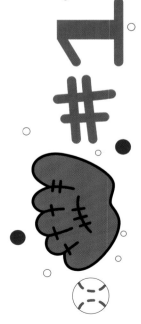

coach's clipboard

Clipboard measures 10×14".
Shown *above* and on *page 119*.

MATERIALS
- Tracing paper and masking tape
- 10×14" clear acrylic clipboard
- Red, white, blue, brown, and black permanent paint pens

INSTRUCTIONS

Use warm, soapy water to wash the clipboard, removing any fingerprints; rinse and dry well. Trace the pattern, *left*, onto tracing paper; cut out, leaving a ⅛" margin around the design. Position and tape the traced design to the back of the clipboard along the bottom edge.

Use red for "#1 Coach," brown for the glove and bat, and white for the baseballs. Use black to outline the glove and to add details to the glove and bag. Use red for the stitch lines on the baseballs. Use red, white, and blue for the pom-poms. Use blue to write the team members' names along the side edges. Repeat the design motifs along the top of the clipboard as desired. Fill in the areas between the names with red stars and blue and white dots. Use blue to write the team's name and the year on the clipboard.❤

Designer: Cut-It-Up
Photographer: Craig Anderson

more
THAN A
box

**Above and far right:
Waxed Paper Wraps
start on *page 136*.**

You've put plenty of *love*
into making a gift from the heart.
Now it's time to consider
the *presentation.*
More than a box covered in
wrapping paper and tied with
a bow, these *innovative*
containers will be saved,
used, and treasured as much as
the gift inside.

The inexpensive envelopes and sacks shown here are as close as
your *kitchen* cupboards, sewing basket, and backyard!
Just sandwich thin, flat items between two pieces of *waxed* paper
and press with an *iron.* Metallic threads, feathers, and garden
flowers were used on the items at *right,* and crayon bits,
embroidery threads, and rickrack for the ones *above.*

Acorn Cracker
starts on *page 138.*

The next time you have a little *tidbit* to wrap, tube it! Trim a
paper-towel tube to size, slip the gift *inside,* then *roll* it in
pretty paper and cellophane with raffia ties at the ends.

Crazy-Quilt Bag
starts on *page 136.*

With a *package* this pretty, who'd believe the "real" gift is on
the inside? Thrill some lucky recipient with this *crazy-quilt* drawstring
bag, *left. Embellished* Victorian-style in lace appliqués,
buttons, and delicate metallic threads, it makes the perfect
dressing for a very special gift.

MORE THAN A BOX

Pressed Flowers
start on *page 138.*

Spring flowers *bloom* again and again when the magic
of technology is coupled with the old-fashioned art of
flower pressing. Once you've completed a pressed
flower design, transform it to a size that
befits your *gift.*

All thumbs when it comes to *wrapping* gifts?
Rather than fuss over a poorly wrapped package,
create one that's neat as a pin, *right.* With *one trip* to your
scrapbooking store, you'll find everything you need:
gabled house boxes and die-cuts
to suit every gift-giving *season.*

Gabled Boxes
start on *page 139*.

A Gift For You

Baby

surprise · enjoy · happy · hooray

1+1=2

Mrs.
Spears

Dog-Gone Tote Bag
starts on *page 140.*

Bow-WOW! What a terrific way to wrap up Fido's birthday treats!
This *no-sew* bag is constructed from a single piece of transparent
vinyl and assembled with *grommets.* Its "ribbon" handle
is really a brand new *leash.*

**Triangular Fishing Box
starts on *page 139.***

A simple *papier-mâché* box becomes
tabletop art when it's handled this creatively.
The alluring triangle container, *above,*
features an enlarged color photocopy on
the lid that's aged in *crackle* finish.
Then the box is hinged and trimmed in
twine threaded with real *fishing* lures
(the hooks removed).

waxed paper wraps

Shown *above* and on *pages 128–129*.

MATERIALS

- Iron and ironing board
- Brown-paper grocery bags
- Waxed paper
- Fillers, such as dried or fresh flowers, leaves, grasses, clover, and star glitter; guinea feathers, peacock feathers, seed beads, and gold glitter; crayon shavings, rickrack, and embroidery floss
- Small brown-paper bags and envelopes for patterns
- Double-stick tape
- Decorative-edge paper scissors
- Decorative thread, cording, or ribbon
- Needle
- Paper punch

INSTRUCTIONS

Open the grocery bags flat and cover the ironing board with them. Pull out two 30" lengths of waxed paper. Place the desired fillers between the two sheets of waxed paper. Cover the layered waxed paper with more brown paper; press with a hot, dry iron.

To make a bag, fold the layered waxed paper, using a small paper bag as a pattern. Adjust the width and length of the waxed paper as needed. Adhere the edges with double-stick tape. Use decorative-edge paper scissors to finish the open edge of the bag. Punch holes through the bag and tie the bag closed with decorative thread, cording, or ribbon, using one of the filler items in the closure if desired.

To make an envelope, cut the layered waxed paper, using an envelope as a pattern. Adhere the edges with double-stick tape. To close, thread a needle with decorative thread and sew the top flap to the back of the envelope.

To make a clutch-type bag or folder, fold the layered waxed paper, creating a top flap. Punch holes through all layers along the open edges. Knot one end of rickrack or ribbon and thread through the punched holes to sew the open edges closed. ♥

Designer: Laura Collins
Photographers: Scott Little and Perry Struse

crazy-quilt bag

Bag measures 6¼×7½". Shown on *page 130*.

MATERIALS

- 8½×11" piece of muslin
- Tracing paper
- Erasable marker
- 8 or more assorted scraps of white and beige fancy fabrics including satin, lace, velvet, taffeta, and brocade
- Assorted 4mm and 7mm silk ribbons
- Cotton, silk, and metallic embroidery floss
- Assorted beads, charms, and buttons
- Size 26 tapestry needle
- Beading needle
- 8½×11" piece of white or beige moiré taffeta
- 2—8½×11" pieces of lining fabric
- 1 yard of white ¼"-diameter satin cording
- 4—½" diameter beads
- Fabric glue
- White sewing thread

INSTRUCTIONS

All seams are ¼".

bag front

Trace the pattern onto tracing paper. Tape it to a light box or brightly lit window. Place the muslin over the pattern. Trace the outline with an erasable marker. Do not cut out yet.

Lay the muslin on a work surface. Select two small fancy fabric scraps (about 2×3") that have at least one straight edge each. Pin one scrap, right side up, in the center of the muslin. With right side down, align the straight edge of the second piece with the first. Stitch ¼" from the straight edge. Press the second right side up.

Select a third fancy fabric scrap that is long enough to cover one raw edge of the first two joined scraps. Align it, face down, at the edge of the first two scraps and stitch using a ¼" seam allowance. Trim the first two scraps even with the edge of the third one. Press the third scrap right side up. Continue adding pieces following the numbers on the pattern until the bag outline is completely covered.

embroidery

Use the assorted ribbons, flosses, beads, lace, buttons, and charms to embellish the seams between the shapes and the centers. If desired,

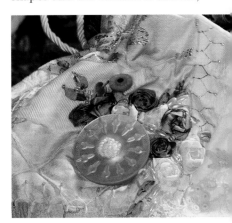

use the stitches shown in the diagrams on *page 157*. Secure lace and beads using tiny hidden stitches. Keep large buttons and trim free of the casing lines.

bag assembly

Cut out the tracing paper pattern and lay it on the pieced bag. Cut out the bag along the outside edges. Use the tracing paper pattern to cut one back from the moiré taffeta and two lining pieces from the lining fabric.

If necessary, use the erasable marker to remark the casing lines on the bag front and moiré back. Pin bag front and back together, right sides facing, and sew along the sides and back, leaving each side open between the dots for the casing. Turn right side out and press.

With right sides together, sew the lining pieces together, leaving a 3" opening at the bottom. Do not turn. Slip the bag into the lining (right sides will be together) and align the raw edges at the top. Sew around the top. Turn right side out through the opening in the lining. Hand-stitch the lining opening closed.

Stitch around the top of the bag on the casing lines. Cut two 12" pieces of white satin cording. Starting on one side, thread one piece of cording through the casing all the way around the bag. Repeat with the second piece of cord, beginning on the opposite side. Add a ½" bead to each cord end and tie a knot. Treat the end of the knots with fabric glue to prevent fraying. Cut an 11" piece of the same white cording and sew the ends to the top inside of the bag at both sides to create a wrist strap. ♥

Designer: Lydia Talton
Photographer: Perry Struse

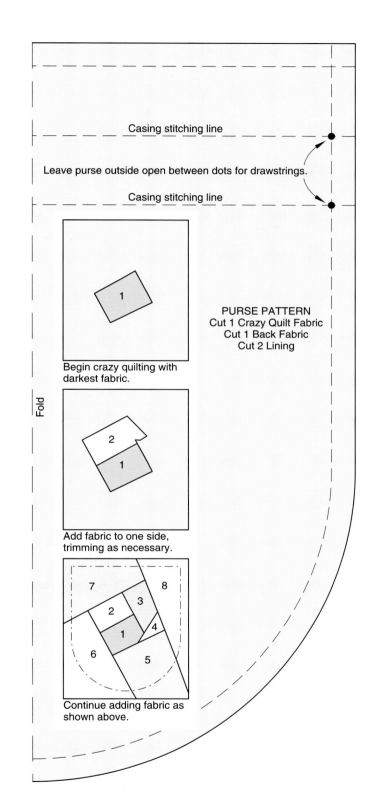

Casing stitching line

Leave purse outside open between dots for drawstrings.

Casing stitching line

Fold

PURSE PATTERN
Cut 1 Crazy Quilt Fabric
Cut 1 Back Fabric
Cut 2 Lining

1

Begin crazy quilting with darkest fabric.

2
1

Add fabric to one side, trimming as necessary.

7   8
2 3
1 4
6   5

Continue adding fabric as shown above.

acorn cracker

Shown *above* and on *page 131.*

MATERIALS

- Paper towel tube
- 1 sheet of decorative paper
- 2 colors of contrasting paper
- Double-stick tape
- Leaf paper punch
- Crafts glue
- Clear cellophane wrap
- Raffia
- Acorn die-cut
- Marking pen

INSTRUCTIONS

Cut the paper towel tube in half. Cover the tube with decorative paper, using double-stick tape to secure. From contrasting paper, cut a 1½" wide strip long enough to go around the tube. Punch out four leaves from contrasting paper; glue the leaves onto the strip. Tape the strip around the center of the tube. Place the gift in the tube. Wrap clear cellophane around the tube, leaving excess on each end. Tie raffia around the cellophane wrap close to the tube. For the gift tag, use a marking pen to write the recipient's name on the die cut; tie with raffia to one end of the tube.❤

Designer: Suzanne State
Photographer: Craig Anderson

pressed flowers

Finished card is 5½" tall. Shown on *page 132.*

MATERIALS

- Purchased flower press or thick telephone book and other large books for weights
- Fresh flowers, herbs, and greens
- Scrapbooking or other colored paper
- Paint pens
- Glue stick
- Color photocopier
- Brown paper bag
- Raffia, ribbon or tasseled cord
- Paper punch

INSTRUCTIONS

Arrange and dry the flowers in the flower press or between the pages of the telephone book following the suggestions *opposite.*

For the purple card, gift tag, and bag, fold a sheet of colored paper into quarters to form a card. Glue pressed flowers onto the front of the card. Use paint pens to draw a simple border. Reduce the design on a color photocopier to make a gift tag. Enlarge it to fit a gift bag.

For gift tags and bookmark, *right,* cut colored paper to the appropriate size. Glue on flowers as desired. Punch a hole, and add ribbon, raffia, or a tasseled cord.❤

Designer: Arlene Cano
Photographer: Craig Anderson

PRESSING FLOWERS

Learn the basics of pressing flowers for great results every time.

- Pick flowers early in the morning.

- Press flowers immediately after picking. Many flowers, particularly wildflowers, begin to wilt within minutes.

- Choose flowers that are neither too delicate nor too thick. Varieties that press well include pansies, bachelor's buttons, coreopsis, violets, buttercups, Queen Anne's lace, and the individual flowers from hydrangea clusters.

- Avoid fleshy flowers such as roses, larkspur, sunflowers, coneflowers, and others that are too thick to press almost paper-thin.

- Carefully arrange the petals, leaves, and stems of flowers facedown on a page before turning to another page. Leave several pages between flowers.

- If the stems are thin, leave them on the flowers to add interest to your arrangements. If the stems are thick, use only the flower heads.

- Make sure the flowers don't overlap or touch; otherwise, they'll stick together when they dry.

- Weight with a heavy object or apply pressure to keep the blooms flat.

- Leave flowers undisturbed in the flower press for about three weeks before removing them.

- Consider pressing leaves with unusual shapes. Pressed ferns or autumn leaves add interesting texture and color to arrangements.

gabled boxes

Finished boxes are about 9" tall. Shown on *page 133*.

MATERIALS

- Gable-top box
- Assorted colored papers
- Scissors
- Two-sided tape
- Scissors
- Assorted die-cuts
- Permanent paint pens

INSTRUCTIONS

Cut desired papers to fit the sides of the box and apply with tape. Arrange die-cuts on the box sides and secure with tape. Use the paint pens to write a message on the box. ❤

Designer: Cut-It-Up
Photographer: Craig Anderson

triangular fishing box

Box is 3½" tall with a 9×9×9" triangular base. Shown on *pages 135* and *140*.

MATERIALS

- Black and white photograph
- 3½"-tall, 9"-wide triangular papier-mâché box
- Delta Soft Tints Matte Sealer and Glaze
- Delta Two-Step Fine-Crackle Finish
- Brown antiquing medium
- Interior/exterior satin finish
- Sponge brush
- Crafts glue
- Crafts knife
- Electric drill and ⅛" drill bit
- Five fishing lures with hooks removed
- Twine or cording

Delta Ceramcoat Colors
- AO Adobe 2046
- MU Mudstone 2488

Delta Soft Tints
- BR Brick Red 3112
- BU Burnt Umber 3113
- DG Dark Green 3119
- GY Golden 3101
- RB Royal 3116
- RG Rouge 03107
- TQ Turquoise 03118

INSTRUCTIONS

cover the box

Make a photocopy of your photograph, enlarging or reducing the image as necessary. The photocopy should be slightly larger than the lid of the box.

Using the sponge brush, base-coat the rim of the box lid MU and the base of the box AO. Let the paint dry.

Apply glue to the back of the photocopy using the sponge brush. Position the photocopy on top of the lid, and smooth it with your fingers to eliminate air bubbles. Let the lid dry slightly, and use the crafts knife to trim the excess paper flush with

Continued

triangular fishing box

the edges of the lid. Apply a coat of matte sealer and glaze over the photocopy; let the lid dry.

Color the photocopy with tinted water as follows. Place a small amount of water in a container. Touch the tip of the sponge brush into the Soft Tints paint of choice, and dip the brush into the water. Add more water as necessary until the color is very light. When the tinted photocopy is completely dry, brush on another coat of matte sealer and glaze.

Apply the first coat of the two-step crackle finish to the box. Allow it to dry for at least 20 minutes, and brush on a thin coat of the second step of the crackle finish. Let it dry overnight.

Brush on and then wipe off a coat of brown antique finish with paper towels; let the finish dry. Then apply a coat of interior/exterior satin finish.

finish

Using the crafts knife, cut into the lid from the bottom of the rim to the top at the two back corners, creating a hinge. Measure and mark five holes

on the hinge, spacing them 2" apart and marking the first and last holes ½" from each end. With the lid on the base of the box, drill through the marked holes on the hinge and through the base.

On the top of the lid, about ¼" from the back (hinge) edge, measure and mark four holes, spacing them 2" apart and marking the first and last holes 1½" from the ends. Drill the holes in the top of the lid. Referring to the photograph, *left,* drill two holes in the front point of the lid, one on each side, for the handle. On the left and right sides of the base, measure and mark three pairs of holes 3" apart and 1½" from the top edge (allow ¼" between the two holes in each pair). Drill the holes.

Knot one end of an 18" length of twine. Thread the other end through the first hole at the right side of the hinge, through the corresponding hole in the base, and then through the hole in the top of the lid. Bring the twine around to the second hole in the hinge, and repeat the threading

sequence. Secure the twine with a knot on the inside of the base.

Tie one end of a 24" length of twine through the first two holes on the left side of the base at the back edge. Thread a lure on the twine, and push the twine through the third hole and up through the fourth hole. Add another lure, and repeat the threading sequence. Wrap the twine around the front point of the box, and thread it through the first hole on the right side of the base. Continue the threading sequence to the back edge. Securing the twine with a large overhand knot.

For the handle, thread a lure on a short length of twine. Push the ends of the twine through the holes on the front corner of the lid, and knot them on the inside. ❤

Designer: Nancy Tribolet
Photographer: Doug Smith

dog-gone tote bag

Bag is 8×8×12". Shown *below* and on *page 134*.

MATERIALS
- 1 yard of 54" frosted sheet vinyl
- 20—⅜" brass grommets
- ⅜" grommet pliers
- 2—1"-diameter D-rings (or size to fit leash)
- 4" of beaded chain with connector
- Dog leash
- 6" of jute
- 4" compressed dog bone
- Drill with ⅛" drill bit
- 4mm white corrugated plastic board
- Large piece of scrap cardboard
- Crafts knife and cutting mat or scissors
- Fine-line marker

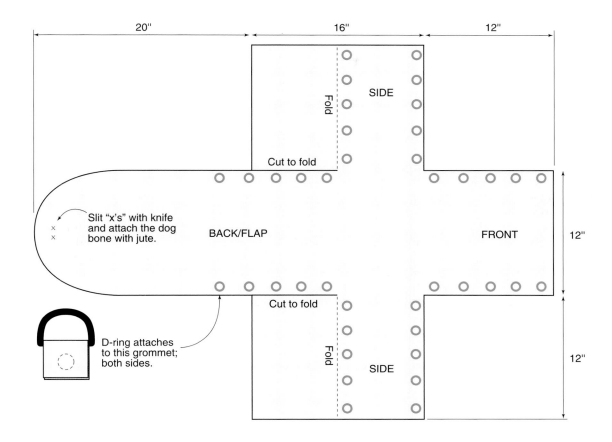

20" 16" 12"

SIDE

Fold

Cut to fold

Slit "x's" with knife
and attach the dog
bone with jute.

BACK/FLAP

FRONT

12"

D-ring attaches
to this grommet;
both sides.

Cut to fold

Fold

SIDE

12"

INSTRUCTIONS

Use the dimensions on the diagram, *above*, to make a template or draw an outline onto the vinyl. Make a template by transferring the bag outline to the scrap cardboard. On a large work surface, lay the sheet vinyl on the cutting mat and the cardboard template on the vinyl. Use the crafts knife to cut around the template, moving the mat as you cut. Or trace the outline of the bag onto the vinyl with a fine line marker and cut out with scissors.

From the vinyl scraps, cut two 1×3" strips for the D-ring connectors. Fold one 1×3" strip around the flat side of each D-ring; set aside.

With the marker make a small circle at each grommet mark and the Xs for the dog-bone fastener.

Carefully slash the vinyl along the "cut to fold" lines. Then fold along the lines indicated on the pattern, and crease with your fingers on the fold line. Bring the grommeted edge of one double-layer side to the grommeted edge of the front. With the grommet pliers punch a hole through all three layers at each grommet mark and attach a grommet. Repeat with the other side.

Bring the folded edge of one side to the back/flap. Insert the ends of the D-ring connectors between the side and the back/flap at the top grommet position. Punch a hole and attach a grommet through all five layers. Attach the remaining grommets along that edge and repeat on the other edge.

Use the crafts knife to cut one 7×11" and two 5¼×12" pieces of corrugated

plastic. Place the 7×11" piece in the bottom of the bag. Insert one 5¼×12" piece between the vinyl layers on each side.

Use the drill and ⅛" drill bit to drill two holes in the center of the dog bone about 1" apart. With the crafts knife, cut small ⅛"-tall Xs about 1" apart in the location indicated on the pattern. Thread the jute through the drilled holes and the Xs to attach the dog bone to the flap.

Fold the leash in half lengthwise and attach both ends to one D-ring. Thread the beaded chain through the fold and the other D-ring. Connect the ends of the chain.♥

Designer: Carrie Topp
Photographers: Marcia Cameron and Scott Little

Stenciled Grape Tray starts on *page 149*.

ENJOYING A
new
home

Whether, new digs means a first *apartment,* a new *house,* or a retirement *condo,* a handmade gift magnifies your good wishes to the happy home finder.

This lovely gift *carries* all your best wishes with it. Like an old tin tray, the 9×12-inch wooden *beauty, left,* wears its "age" well. Painted and crackled with a brush-on finish, it's adorned in a *vine* of softly stenciled grapes.

Quilt Clock
starts on *page 150.*

Know anyone with a penchant for *patchwork* and fabrics?
  She'll fall "thread"-over-heals in love with this painted wall clock, *above.*
It comes as a kit with all the clockworks included. You just paint on
  the *scraps* and the faux *fabric* background.

Extend a warm *welcome* with a wooden birdhouse and clay pot,
  that take their painting cue from *Monet,* using impressionistic dabs
of pastel color for their *fragrant* hydrangea blooms.

Hydrangea Clay Pot and Birdhouse
start on *page 153.*

**Bluebird
Painted Box
starts on
*page 147.***

Bold and colorful *geometries* cover every inch of what was once a plain
wooden box. Raised from the table surface on rosy *knob* legs, the lid gets a lift
when a perky wooden *bird* is attached for a handle.

bluebird painted box

Box measures 7¼×5×4". Shown *opposite*.

MATERIALS

- Tracing paper
- Graphite or transfer paper
- Purchased unfinished 7¼×5×2¾" wooden box
- 4—1½"-diameter ball feet
- ¾×2½×4½"pine
- Scrollsaw
- Electric rotary tool
- Drill
- Medium- and fine-grit sandpaper
- Tack cloth
- Wood sealer
- Brushes: #5 round, #1 script liner, #6 shader, ¾" glaze

- Blue painter's tape
- 5-minute epoxy
- 1½" length of 19-gauge wire
- FolkArt Outdoor Satin Sealer

Plaid FolkArt Colors
- LM Lemonade 904
- LC Licorice 938
- LF Light Fuchsia 688
- PW Periwinkle 404
- WW Wicker White 901

Plaid FolkArt Artists' Pigments
- AQ Aqua 481

INSTRUCTIONS

prepare the pieces

Trace the bird pattern, *left*, onto tracing paper. Use graphite paper to transfer the outline of the bird onto the ¾" pine. Cut out the shape with a scrollsaw. Use the electric rotary tool to shape and round the edges of the bird. Drill a hole in the bottom of the bird and through the center of the box lid to accommodate the 19-gauge wire.

Sand all surfaces of the wooden pieces with medium- and then fine-grit sandpaper. Remove the sanding dust with a tack cloth. Apply wood sealer to all surfaces, and let the sealer

Continued

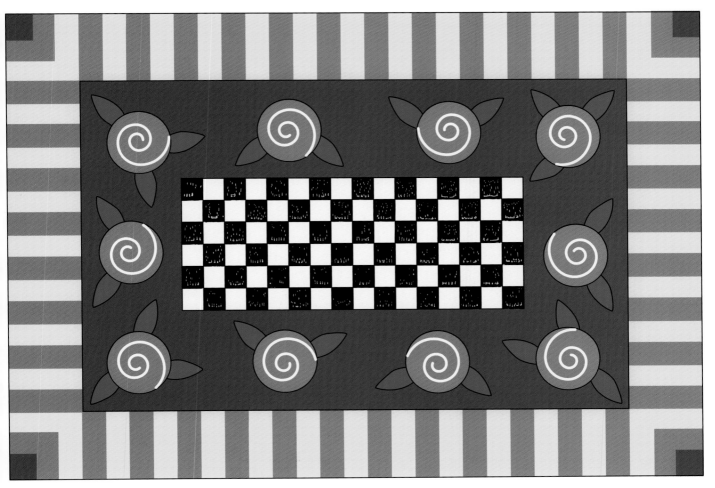

BOX TOP

BOX SIDE

bluebird painted box

dry. Lightly sand again with fine-grit sandpaper, and wipe clean with a tack cloth.

paint

Refer to the photograph on *page 146* and patterns as guides for placement and details. Avoid painting areas where they'll be joined later, as epoxy does not bond permanently to painted surfaces.

Base-coat the ball feet and inside the box base LF.

Use blue tape to mask off all but the checkerboard areas, creating a ½"-wide band on the sides of the base sides and a center rectangle on the lid. Use WW and the glaze brush to paint these areas, the sides of the lid, and the bottom of the base. Let the paint dry; apply a second coat. When the paint is dry, remove the tape. Use the #6 shader and LC to paint the checks on all WW areas, except the bottom of the box.

When the checks are completely dry, use tape to mask off all but the blue areas, creating a 1"-wide band on the base sides and a frame around the checkerboard rectangle on the lid. Use PW and the glaze brush to paint these areas and the bird. Let the paint dry; apply a second coat. When the paint is dry, remove the tape.

Use tape to mask off all but the yellow areas, creating a ¾"-wide outside border on the lid and a ⅛"-wide line on the base sides. Use the glaze brush and LM to paint the unmasked areas and the bird's beak. Let the paint dry; apply a second coat. When the paint is dry, remove the tape.

Mask off the narrow unpainted area at the top of the base sides; apply two coats of LF. Remove the tape when the paint is dry.

Use the #5 round brush and LF to paint the flowers on the PW areas. When the flowers are dry, use the liner and LM to add a swirl on each flower. Paint the leaves with AQ and the round brush. Use the handle end of a paintbrush and LM to add the dots between the flowers on the sides of the box base. Use the #6 shader and LF to paint the stripes on the outer border of the lid. Use PW to paint a small square at each lid corner. Dot the bird's eyes with LC, using the handle end of a paintbrush.

finish the box

Epoxy the feet to the bottom of the box. Epoxy one end of 19-gauge wire length in the hole at the bottom of the bird. Insert wire through the predrilled hole in the lid; bend the wire to secure the bird to the lid.

Apply the outdoor satin sealer to all surfaces of the box. Let the sealer dry and apply a second coat. ♥

Designer: Sandra McCooey
Photographer: Perry Struse

stenciled grape tray

Tray measures 9×12". Shown on *page 142*.

MATERIALS

- Walnut Hollow 9×12" tray #3575
- Medium- and fine-grit sandpaper
- Tack cloth
- Aleene's Enhancers: All-Purpose Primer, Mosaic Crackle Medium-Step 1, Mosaic Crackle Activator-Step 2, and Matte Varnish
- American Traditional Grapevine stencil (BL-549) or stencil acetate film, crafts knife, and manicure scissors
- Low-tack masking tape
- Brushes: 1" flat, ¼" flat, stencil brushes in assorted sizes

Continued on *page 150*.

grape stenciled tray

Continued from *page 149*.

Aleene's Premium Coat Acrylic Paint
- BG   Burgundy OC186
- DL   Deep Lavender OC158
- DV   Deep Violet OC164
- HG   Hunter Green OC188
- IV   Ivory OC179
- SG   Dusty Sage OC135
- YO   Yellow Ochre OC184

INSTRUCTIONS

prepare and paint the tray

Sand all surfaces of the tray with medium- and then fine-grit sandpaper. Remove the sanding dust with a tack cloth. Apply All-Purpose Primer to all surfaces of the tray; let the sealer dry. Sand the tray again with fine-grit sandpaper, and wipe clean with a tack cloth.

Using the 1" flat brush, base-coat the back of the tray with SG. Let the paint dry.

Mix Mosaic Crackle Medium-Step 1 with SG, following the manufacturer's instructions. Apply one heavy coat of the mixture to the front of the tray; let the mixture dry for 30 minutes. Paint the top of the tray with IV; let the paint dry. Apply a thick coat of the Mosaic Crackle Activator-Step 2. Let the activator dry for 24 to 48 hours at room temperature or until thoroughly dry.

Using the ¼" flat brush, paint the edge of the tray with HG; let the paint dry.

stencil the tray

If you're cutting your own stencil, transfer the stencil pattern, *page 149,* onto stencil acetate film. Cut out the stencil using a crafts knife and manicure scissors.

To stencil, dab end of a dry stencil brush lightly into paint. Swirl the bristles onto a paper towel to remove excess paint and distribute the paint evenly on the bristles. There should be very little paint on the brush. Pounce or swirl brush over stencil openings. When using more than one color for a stencil motif, start with the lightest color and work to the darkest color. Using one brush for each color of paint eliminates the muddying of colors. Paint may be rinsed from the brush before applying another color to the motif. Be sure to remove all of the moisture from the brush by rubbing it out onto an old terry towel.

Position one of the grape cluster motifs on the left side of the tray, referring to the photograph, *pages 142–143,* for placement. Tape the stencil in place; use masking tape to block out parts of the stencil that won't be used. Stencil as directed above, beginning with YO to accent the tops of some grapes and the center of some leaves. Use BG to stencil the vine, some of the grapes, and the leaf tips. Use DV to stencil the grapes. Stencil DL to accent the leaves and to create shadows and darker areas on the stem and grapes. Stencil HG on the remainder of the leaves and over the BG on the stem, creating a brown. Remove the stencil and allow to dry.

Reposition the second grape cluster motif on the right side of the tray, overlapping the first motif to create a connected vine. Tape in place and stencil as before; remove the stencil.

finish the tray

When the paint is completely dry, apply 2 to 3 coats of Matte Varnish to all surfaces of the tray, letting dry thoroughly between each coat. ❤

Designer: Barbara Swanson
Photographer: Perry Struse

quilt clock

Clock measures 11½" square.
Shown on *page 144.*

MATERIALS
- Tracing paper
- 11½" square clock frame, clock mechanism, and batteries
- Medium- and fine-grit sandpaper
- Tack cloth
- Wood sealer
- Graphite or transfer paper
- Stylus
- Toothpicks
- Painter's tape
- Fine-tip permanent black marking pen, such as Pigma .01
- Matte acrylic spray
- Brushes: #10 and #12 shader; 10/0 and #4 liner; 1" foam

DecoArt Americana Colors
- AV   Avocado DA52
- BD   Burgundy Wine DA22
- BK   Buttermilk DA3
- BY   Blueberry DA37
- CA   Calico Red DA20
- CB   Country Blue DA41
- DM   Deep Midnight Blue DA166
- EG   Evergreen DA82
- HB   Honey Brown DA163
- SN   Sand DA4

INSTRUCTIONS

prepare the clock

Sand all surfaces of the clock with medium- and then fine-grit sandpaper. Remove the sanding dust with a tack cloth. Apply sealer to all surfaces of

CLOCKFACE
PATTERN

paint the clock

Refer to the photograph, *page 144,* and pattern, *above* and on *page 152,* as guides for placement, shading, and details. Use the foam or shader brushes to base-coat, using the size that best fits the area. Float shading with the shader brushes. Apply details with the liner brushes. Use the stylus, the handle end of a paintbrush, or the tip of a toothpick to make dots.

Trace the patterns onto tracing paper. Use graphite paper to transfer the outlines of the quilt block onto the clock, centering the block on the

the clock; let the sealer dry. Sand the clock again with fine-grit sandpaper, and wipe clean with a tack cloth.

clock. Don't transfer the details yet, you'll base-coat over them.

Base-coat the background around the quilt block SN; mottle with HB. Let the paint dry.

Using painter's tape, mask off the background area. Use CB to base-coat square #1, triangles #3 and #5, and side points #10, #11, #14, and #15; float BY shading along the edges of each shape. Base-coat squares #2, #4, #6, and #8 SN; float HB shading along the edges of each square. Base-coat triangles #7 and #9 BY; float DM shading along the edges of each triangle. Base-coat side points #12, #13, #16, and #17 AV; float EG shading along the edges of each side point. Base-coat the background triangles of the quilt

block BK; float HB shading along the edges of each triangle. Use BD to base-coat the narrow border around the quilt block. Let the paint dry; remove tape.

Freehand paint the details or use graphite paper to transfer the details onto the clock. Details not specifically mentioned below are added later with fine-tip black permanent marking pen. For triangles #3 and #5, use a #4 liner and DM to paint the circles and line swirls; add HB dots around the circles. For the CB side points, use EG and DM to paint the lines and swirls. For the SN squares, use CA to paint the lines, three-dot clusters, stripes and swirls; dot the intersecting lines with

Continued

BACKGROUND
PATTERN

quilt clock

BK and dot the ends of swirls with HB. For triangles #7 and #9, make three-dot clusters with BK. For the AV side points, use HB and EG to paint the lines and stripes.

To add the floral background, use a liner brush and HB to paint the flower stems and leaves. Paint the open flower petals CB and the flower buds BY. Dot the open flower centers CA.

Base-coat all surfaces of the clock frame, including the back, with BD.

finishing the clock
Use the fine-tip permanent black marking pen to line draw the details and pen-stitch the background triangles on the quilt block. Let dry for 24 hours before sealing. Spray with matte acrylic sealer according to the manufacturer's instructions. ♥

Designer: Leslie Beck
Photographer: Perry Struse

hydrangea pot

Pot measures 5¼" tall and 7" across.
Shown at *right* and on *page 145*.

MATERIALS

- Tracing paper
- Terra-cotta flower pot
- DecoArt Multi-Purpose Sealer
- Graphite or transfer paper
- Scrap wood
- Krylon 1311 Matte-Finish Spray
- Brushes: #8 filbert, #10 filbert, 10/0
  liner, spatter brush or old toothbrush,
  sponge brush

DecoArt Americana Colors

- AV Avocado DA52
- BT Blue Mist DA178
- EG Evergreen DA82
- OG Olive Green DA56
- TG Teal Green DA107
- TW Titanium White DA1

INSTRUCTIONS

prepare the pot

Wash the pot in warm, soapy water,
rinse thoroughly, and let dry overnight. Apply sealer to both the inside
and outside surfaces of the pot; let
the sealer dry. Apply one or more
additional coats of sealer on the
inside of the pot.

paint the pot

Base-coat the pot TW; let the paint
dry thoroughly.

Trace the pattern, *right,* onto tracing
paper; cut out, leaving a ¼" margin
around the design. Use graphite paper
to transfer the pattern onto the surface.

To paint leaves and flower petals,
load a filbert brush three-fourths of
the way up to the metal ferrule. Press
the tip of the brush to the surface
and let the hairs fan out by applying
pressure. As you slowly let the hairs
return to their natural position, move
the brush forward and slightly rotate
it to the left as you form a point just
before lifting the brush from the
surface. Practice this technique on

scrap wood before painting on the
flower pot. To achieve the best results,
clean your brush from time to time
and do not let paint get into the metal
ferrule of the brush.

Using a #10 filbert brush, base-coat
the large leaves AV using the above
technique. While you still have AV
on the brush, pull one side of the
brush through OG and the other
side through EG. Gently blend
the colors on a clean part of a
palette to soften the line. Go over
the leaves again using the same
technique to add shading and
highlighting. Do not base-coat
the small leaves, just paint as if
shading and highlighting.

Using a #8 filbert brush and
BT, base-coat the large hydrangea
petals around the outer edges of
the flower ball. Continue making
petals, loading the brush first with
BT and then a little TW on the
tip. Make the four-petal flowers
from the outer edges in, increasing
the amount of TW on the brush
to vary the color within the
flower ball.

If desired, make several pale OG
flowers at the center of the flower ball.

Thin OG with water to ink
consistency; use the liner brush
and the diluted paint to make light
squiggles around the hydrangea
flower balls. Use the tip of the liner
brush to make dots at the center of
some of the flowers.

finish the pot

When the paint is completely dry,
spray the painted surfaces of the pot
with matte finish. Dilute OG with
water to ink consistency; dip a spatter
brush or an old toothbrush into the
diluted paint, and flick your thumb
across the bristles to lightly spatter
the painted surfaces of the pot. Thin
TG with water to ink consistency;
spatter the painted surfaces of the pot.
If you are unhappy with the spattering,
spatters can be wiped off while the
paint is still wet.

When the paint is completely dry,
apply another coat of matte finish to
the pot.♥

Designer: Pat Jabcninski
Photographer: Perry Struse

HYDRANGEA POT
Repeat hydrangea pattern five times
around the clay pot.

hydrangea birdhouse

Birdhouse measures 6×8×7".
Shown above and on *page 145*.

MATERIALS
- Tracing paper
- Graphite or transfer paper
- Purchased unfinished wooden birdhouse
- Medium- and fine-grit sandpaper
- Wood filler
- Tack cloth
- Wood sealer
- Crackle medium
- Scrap wood
- Krylon 1311 Matte-Finish Spray
- ½ yard each of 1½"-wide green and lavender sheer ribbons
- Screw eye
- Brushes: #8 filbert, #10 filbert, 10/0 liner, spatter brush or old toothbrush, 2 sponge brushes

DecoArt Americana Colors
- AV Avocado DA52
- DP Dioxazine Purple DA101
- EG Evergreen DA82
- OG Olive Green DA56
- TG Teal Green DA107
- TW Titanium White DA1

INSTRUCTIONS
Trace the patterns, *pages 153 and 155*, onto tracing paper; cut out, leaving a ¼" margin.

prepare the wood
Use wood filler to fill in any nail holes or other irregularities on the birdhouse; let the filler dry.

Sand all surfaces of the birdhouse with medium- and then fine-grit sandpaper. Remove the sanding dust with a tack cloth. Apply wood sealer to all surfaces, and let the sealer dry. Sand again with fine-grit sandpaper, and wipe clean with a tack cloth.

paint the birdhouse
Base-coat the birdhouse TG; let the paint dry thoroughly. Apply a coat of crackle medium to the birdhouse with a sponge brush, applying a heavy coat for large cracks or a light coat for small cracks. Let the crackle medium dry for 2 to 4 hours.

With a sponge brush, apply one coat of TW over the crackle medium, brushing only in one direction. Let the paint dry for at least 2 to 4 hours; the paint will crack as it dries.

To add the flowers, referring to the photograph, select portions of the patterns, *opposite and page 153*, that fit the area you want to paint. Use graphite paper to transfer those patterns onto the surface.

To paint leaves and flower petals, use the technique described for the hydrangea pot on *page 153*.

Using a #10 filbert brush, base-coat the large leaves AV using the above technique. While you still have AV on the brush, pull one side of the brush through OG and the other side through EG. Gently blend the colors on a clean part of a palette to soften the line. Go over the leaves again using the same technique to add shading and highlighting. Do not base-coat the small leaves, just paint as if shading and highlighting.

Using a #8 filbert brush and DP, base-coat the large hydrangea petals around the outer edges of the flower ball. Continue making petals, loading the brush first with DP and then a little TW on the tip. Make the four-petal flowers from the outer edges in, increasing the amount of TW on the brush to vary the color within the flower ball.

If desired, make several pale OG flowers at the center of the flower ball.

Thin OG with water to an ink consistency; use the liner brush and the diluted paint to make light squiggles around the hydrangea flower balls. Use the tip of the liner brush to make dots at the center of some of the flowers.

finish the birdhouse

When the paint is completely dry, spray all surfaces of the birdhouse with matte finish. Dilute OG with water to ink consistency; dip a spatter brush or an old toothbrush into the diluted paint, and flick your thumb across the bristles to lightly spatter all surfaces of the birdhouse. Thin TG with water to ink consistency; spatter all surfaces of the birdhouse. If you are unhappy with the spattering, spatters can be wiped off while the paint is wet.

When the paint is completely dry, apply another coat of matte finish to all surfaces of the birdhouse. Screw the screw eye in the top center of the birdhouse. Align the ends of the two ribbon lengths and tie into a bow through the screw eye. ♥

Designer: Pat Jabczynski
Photographer: Perry Struse

HYDRANGEA BIRDHOUSE

1 1/8" hole

1/4" hole

crafting basics

TRANSFERRING PATTERNS

fabric

Step 1: Use an iron-on transfer pen with dark ink for light-colored fabrics and white ink for dark fabrics. Unless the pattern is printed in reverse, trace it with a pencil onto tracing paper, flip it over, and trace it with an iron-on transfer pen.

Step 2: Position the tracing paper ink side down on your fabric. Using a hot iron without steam, press on top of the paper to transfer the design.

wood

Step 1: Duplicate the pattern by placing tracing paper over the design and tracing over it with pencil.

Step 2: Transfer the design to the project surface by taping down one edge of the traced pattern. Place transfer paper under the pattern, and trace over it again with a stylus or pencil.

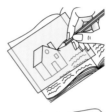

CROCHET

slipknot

Step 1: Hold the tail of the yarn between your left thumb and forefinger. Loop the yarn attached to the ball to form a figure eight.

Step 2: Insert your crochet hook from right to left through the first loop.

Step 3: Pull the tail and the yarn attached to the ball to tighten the loop on the hook. Be careful not to overtighten the loop—tighten it only enough to keep it from falling off the hook.

chain

Make a slipknot about 4" from the end of the yarn and slip the loop onto the crochet hook. Weave the yarn

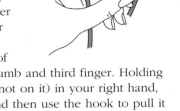

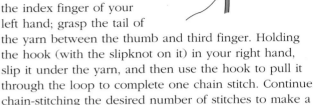

loosely under the pinkie, over the ring finger, under the third finger, and over the index finger of your left hand; grasp the tail of the yarn between the thumb and third finger. Holding the hook (with the slipknot on it) in your right hand, slip it under the yarn, and then use the hook to pull it through the loop to complete one chain stitch. Continue chain-stitching the desired number of stitches to make a foundation chain.

single crochet

Step 1: At the beginning of a row, insert your crochet hook into the second chain from the hook.

Steps 2 and 3: Slip the hook under the yarn, and then use the hook to pull it through the chain. This is called "yarn over" (or "yarn over hook") and is abbreviated as "yo." Notice that there are two loops on the hook.

Steps 4 and 5: Yarn over again, and then pull the loop completely through the two loops on the hook to complete a single crochet. To work the next single crochet, insert your hook into the next chain, and repeat steps 2–5.

double crochet

Step 1: At the beginning of a row, slip the hook under the yarn (yarn over), and insert the hook into the fourth chain from the hook.

Step 2: Yarn over again, and pull the loop through the stitch. There are three loops on the hook.

Step 3: Yarn over, and pull the loop completely through the first two loops on the hook. Notice that two loops remain on the hook.

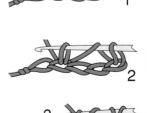

Steps 4 and 5: Yarn over once more, and pull the loop through the remaining two loops on the hook. One loop remains on the hook to complete a double crochet. To work the next double crochet, yarn over and insert your hook into the next chain; repeat steps 2-5.

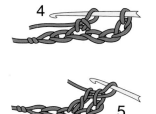

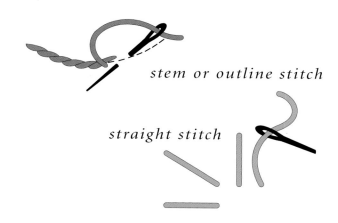

stem or outline stitch

straight stitch

EMBROIDERY STITCHES

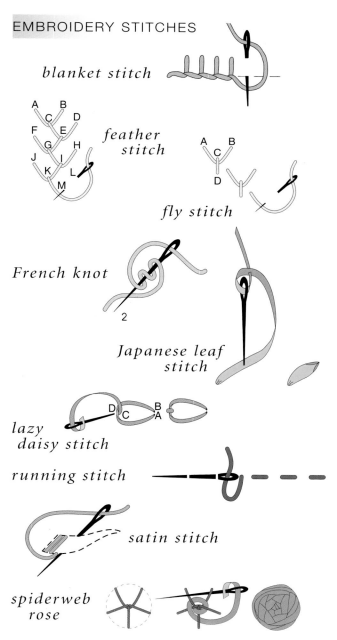

blanket stitch

feather stitch

fly stitch

French knot

Japanese leaf stitch

lazy daisy stitch

running stitch

satin stitch

spiderweb rose

KNITTING

cast on

Step 1: Make a slipknot (see Crochet, *opposite*) leaving a long tail of thread. Holding the knitting needle in your right hand, slide the slipknot onto the knitting needle. Pull gently on the yarn to tighten the slipknot so it doesn't fall off the needle.

Step 2: Hold the yarn attached to the ball in your left hand, slipping it around your thumb and holding it in place with the fingers of your left hand. Arch the thumb slightly to create a little tension.

Step 3: Move the needle to the right of your left thumb, and then slip the needle tip under the strand of yarn in your left palm.

Step 4: Let the yarn slip off your thumb, and pull gently on the yarn to tighten the new stitch on the needle. Repeat steps 2–4 to reach the number of stitches indicated in the project instructions.

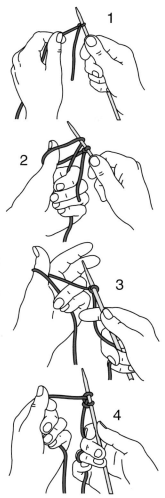

Continued

knit stitch

Step 1: Hold the needle with the cast-on stitches on it in your left hand. Hold the other needle in your right hand. Insert the right-hand needle (RHN) from front to back into the first stitch on the left-hand needle (LHN). Notice that the RHN is behind the LHN.

Step 2: Form a loop by wrapping the yarn under and around the RHN.

Step 3: With the RHN, pull the loop through the stitch on the LHN so the loop is in front of the work. You have just made a new knit stitch, which is on the RHN.

Step 4: With the new stitch on the RHN, slip the first or "old" knit stitch over and off the tip of the LHN. The knit stitch is complete. Notice that the stitch is smooth on the front and that it has a V shape.

purl stitch

Step 1: Hold the needle that has the cast-on stitches on it in your left hand. Hold the other needle in your right hand. With your yarn in front of the work, put the RHN from back to front into the first stitch on the LHN. Note the RHN is in front of the LHN.

Step 2: Form a loop by wrapping the yarn on top of and around the RHN.

Step 3: Bring the RHN under the LHN and pull the loop through the stitch with the RHN onto the LHN to make a new purl stitch. Notice that the RHN will slip behind the LHN as shown.

Step 4: With the new stitch securely on the RHN, slip the first or "old" purl stitch over and off the tip of the LHN. The

purl stitch is complete. Notice that, unlike the smooth knit stitch, the purl stitch has a bump or ridge at its base.

knit slip stitch

To slip a stitch knitwise, insert the right-hand needle in the stitch as if to knit. Then slip the stitch off the left-hand needle and onto the right-hand needle without stitching it. In this case, notice that the stitch becomes twisted.

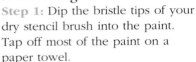
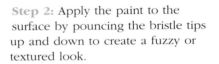
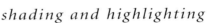

PAINTING

stenciling

Step 1: Dip the bristle tips of your dry stencil brush into the paint. Tap off most of the paint on a paper towel.

Step 2: Apply the paint to the surface by pouncing the bristle tips up and down to create a fuzzy or textured look.

shading and highlighting

Step 1: Select your main color, such as red, and use it to base-coat the surface. Apply your paint with the largest brush that will fit the design area.

Step 2: Shade with a darker color, using the floating technique. Shading makes an area appear to recede, separating it from the surrounding color.

Step 3: Highlight your work by floating a lighter color on the design. Highlighting makes an area appear more prominent, adding dimension.

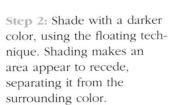
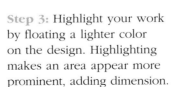

resources

Many materials for the projects in this book can be found in your local crafts, fabric, and specialty stores. Or contact these manufacturers for purchasing information.

NEEDLEWORK

Anchor (J. & P. Coats)
www.coatsandclark.com; Consumer Services Dept., P.O. Box 2706, Greenville, SC 29616.

DMC
www.dmc-usa.com; 10 Port Kearny, South Kearny, NJ 07032.

YLI Corporation
161 W. Main St., Rock Hill, SC 29730; 800/296-8139.

PAINTING

DecoArt
www.decoart.com; 800/367-3043.

Delta Technical Coatings
www.deltacrafts.com; 800/423-4135.

Duncan Products (Aleene's)
www.duncanceramics.com; 5673 E. Shields Ave., Fresno, CA 93727; 559/291-4444.

Plaid Enterprises (FolkArt)
www.plaidonline.com; 800/842-4197.

PROJECTS

tokens of love and friendship
- *Punched Paper Lace:* Paper punches—All Night Media, 800-STAMPED. Beads—The Beadery, 106 Canochet Rd., P.O. Box 178, Hope Valley, RI 02832; Mill Hill Beads, www.millhill.com; 800/447-1332.
- *Glittering Valentines:* Shaker template—Art Gone Wild, 800/945-3980.
- *Felt Heart Mat:* Felt—Kunin Felt, www.kuninfelt.com; 800/292-7900.

anniversaries and weddings
- *Tiny Favor Boxes:* Stamp pads—Colorbox Ink Pads, ClearSnap, P.O. Box 98, Anacortes, WA 98221; Stamps—Stampendous, Inc., www.stampendous.com, 1357 S. Lewis St., Anaheim, CA 92805; Personal Stamp Exchange, 360 Sutton Pl., Santa Rosa, CA 95407; 562/906-1262; River City Rubber Works, 5555 S. Meridian, Wichita, KS 67217; Stamp Your Art Out, 9685 Kenwood Rd., Blue Ash, OH 45242.
- *Picture-Perfect Pillow:* Trims—Flights of Fancy Boutique, www.flightsoffancyboutique.com; 800-530-8745.
- *Decoupaged Corsage Box:* Papier-mâché box—Decorator & Craft Corp.; 428 S. Zelta, Wichita, KS 67207, 316/685-6265.

welcoming the new arrival
- *I Spy Quilt:* 3½"-diameter hexagon templates—Come Quilt With Me, 3903 Avenue I, Brooklyn, NY 11210; 718/377-3652.
- *Shhh…Sign:* Slate—Cape Cod Cooperage, 1150 Queen Anne Rd., Chatham, MA 02633; 508/432-0788.
- *Lacy Blanket Edging:* J. & P. Coats Luster Sheen yarn—Anchor.
- *Ribbon-Embroidered Christening Overlay:* White linen bodice—Adam Original, www.adamoriginal.com; 800/582-ADAM.
- *Transfer-Embellished Children's Clothing:* Chintz Ware and chenille fabrics—Daisy Kingdom, www.daisykingdom.com; 134 NW. 8th Ave, Portland, OR 97209; 503/222-9033. Buttons—Flights of Fancy Boutique. Photo transfers—Ribbon Store, www.ribbonstore.com; 5895 Dunneville, Las Vegas, NV 89118.

gifts kids can make
- *Dad's Travel Kit:* Box—Highsmith Company Inc., P.O. Box 800, Ft. Atkinson, WI 52358. Puzzle template—Creative Xpress, www.creativexpress.com, 800/563-8679.
- *Sewing Box:* Papier-mâché box—Decorator & Craft Corp.

for moms and dads
- *Embellished Button Mirror:* Buttons—Flights of Fancy Boutique.
- *Fishing Lure Box:* Box—Wayne's Wooden Ware; 800/840-1497.

celebrate the holidays
- *Fall Goodie Box:* Box—Cabin Crafters; 800/669-3920.
- *Place Card Treats:* Triangle template—Stamp Your Art Out. Punch and pen—Marvy/Uchida of America, www.uchida.com; 3535 Del Amo Blvd., Torrance, CA, 90503; 310/821-0450. Stickers—Mrs. Grossman's Paper Co., 800/429-4549. Paper edgers—Fiskars, www.fiskars.com; 7811 W. Stewart Ave., Wausau, WI 54401; 715/842-2091.
- *Maple Leaf Favor:* Pens—Marvy/Uchida of America. Ink pads—Printworks Collection, 123 McCann Dr., Santa Fe Springs, CA 90670; 562/906-1262. Stamp—Personal Stamp Exchange.

making the grade
- *Apple Box:* Box—Cabin Crafters, 1225 W. First St., Nevada, IA 50201. Orders only: 800/669-3920.

more than a box
- *Triangular Fishing Box:* Papier-mâché box—Decorator & Craft Corp.
- *Gabled Boxes:* Gable-top boxes and die-cuts—Cut-It-Up, www.scrapramento.com; P.O. Box 30 Dutch Flats, CA 95714; 916/646-4646.

enjoying a new home
- *Stenciled Grape Tray:* Tray—Walnut Hollow, 1409 State Road 23, Dodgeville, WI 53533; 608/935-2341. Stencil and stencil brushes—The Stencil Outlet, 800-2-Stencil.

Handmade gifts—crafted with pride and given with love—are truly *Gifts from the Heart*™.

Better Homes and Gardens®

gifts from the heart™

editor-in-chief	BEVERLY RIVERS

creative director	DANIEL MASINI
senior editor	EVE MAHR
associate art director	CARRIE TOPP
editorial coordinator	CAROL LINNAN
editorial project coordinator	BARBARA HICKEY
administrative assistant	MARY JOHNSON
contributing writers	LAURA COLLINS, RHONDA MATTUS
copy editors	SUSAN J. KLING, DEBRA MORRIS SMITH, AND MARIA DURYEE
contributing illustrators	MARCIA CAMERON, BARBARA GORDON, AND CHRIS NEUBAUER GRAPHICS
photo stylist	LENNY HOUTS

publishing director	WILLIAM R. REED
publisher	MAUREEN RUTH
marketing manager	BECKY NASH
promotion supervisor	MERRI MOSER
business manager	CATHY BELLIS
production director	DOUGLAS M. JOHNSTON
book production managers	PAM KVITNE
	MARJORIE J. SCHENKELBERG
marketing assistant	MEGAN THOMPSON

vice president
JERRY WARD

chairman and CEO
WILLIAM T. KERR

chairman of the executive committee
E.T. MEREDITH III

meredith publishing group

publishing group president	STEVE LACY
president magazine group	JERRY KAPLAN
creative services	ELLEN DE LATHOUDER
manufacturing	BRUCE HESTON
consumer marketing	KARLA JEFFRIES
operations	DEAN PIETERS
finance	MAX RUNCIMAN

For book editorial questions, write:
Better Homes and Gardens® Gifts from the Heart™ • 1716 Locust St., Des Moines, IA 50309-3023